Don't Be Fooled!

A Citizen's Guide to News and Information in the Digital Age

John H. McManus Ph.D.

THE UNVARNISHED PRESS

Cover art by Chris Hall, Ampersand Visual Communications

ISBN: 0615626475

ISBN-13: 978-0615626475

This book can be purchased in either print or digital form. Further information is available at http://DontBeFooled.info

THE UNVARNISHED PRESS
297 N. Frances St.
Sunnyvale, CA 94086
USA

408-773-8711

For Sister Angela Mary Parker I.H.M. and all the nuns

who dedicated their lives to molding lumps of clay

into vessels for wisdom.

CONTENTS

A Confession of Bias

In this book I argue that information-providers should be transparent so you'll know when to power up your skepticism shields.

Nelson Mandela once said "where you stand depends on where you sit." Without being aware of it, we absorb biases from where we are situated in society. Our race, gender, generation, geography, class and nationality each have a great deal to do with how we perceive the world. So let me alert you to where I'm coming from.

With no say in the matter, I was born melanin-challenged to Irish-American parents, a drop in the libidinal tidal wave that followed World War II. My dad was a labor lawyer, a man of stubborn principle who refused to join the country club down the street from our home in the comfortable suburbs of Washington DC until it admitted both blacks and Jews. My mom was a housewife made desperate by five children. I was educated by a tribe of women clad from head to toe in black-and-blue-chadors. Their habits were medieval. Each carried a chain studded with heavy black beads. They called themselves the Sisters of the Immaculate Heart of Mary. Despite their asynchronous appearance, they were wonderful, caring women and master teachers to whom I owe more than I can repay.

I came of age late in the 1960s. I missed Woodstock and the Summer of Love. I dropped aspirin rather than acid, and then only to ease hangovers. Marijuana inflamed my asthma. I attended a (then) all-male institution run by men in black dresses, the Jesuits. After graduating from Holy Cross, I headed west to the University of Michigan for a masters degree in journalism (and a minor in rugby) and a decade later to Stanford for a doctorate in communication.

As a child of '60s, I wanted to change the world. And still do. That's why I became a journalist. I worked as a newspaper reporter in the South because what I most wanted to change was racism. I worked for papers in rural, and later, coastal Virginia and in South Carolina, writing as often as I was allowed about structural issues of class and color. (I am my father's son.) In 1983, I resigned from the *Virginian-Pilot*, packed my family and all our belongings in a yellow Ryder truck, "the lemon of wrath," and camped from Norfolk, Virginia across the country to Palo Alto, California to finish my formal education. Seduced by weather and surf, I still live in the San Francisco Bay Area.

I left daily journalism partly to report a story about it. In various newsrooms, I kept slamming into commercial barriers that my graduate education at Michigan hadn't warned me about. It was the subject of my doctoral dissertation and later a book about how market forces influence the news — *Market-Driven Journalism: Let the Citizen Beware?*

After Stanford, I taught journalism for a decade at several universities. Naively, I thought I had escaped market pressures, but inevitably I was fired for willfully mistaking my customers for students. I flouted departmental enrollment targets, remorselessly inflicting on hapless students the grades they earned, thus risking their defection to more accommodating majors, or — God forefend — entirely driving away a tuition. I callously returned essays bleeding corrections. I failed to encourage my students' creative spelling, syntax, and grammar. In short, I was a disaster as a post-modern professor.

Riding the boot, I left the classroom to design research for the Berkeley Media Studies Group. In 2000, from my bedroom in Silicon Valley, I launched Grade the News, an online effort to do for news in the Bay Area what *Consumer Reports* does for toaster ovens. Attracting funding from the Gerbode, Ford and Knight foundations, I moved it to Stanford and later to San Jose State University.

The idea for this book took shape while evaluating the most popular Bay Area newspapers and TV newscasts at Grade the News. I could see mainstream media deteriorating and the uneven beginnings of a new journalism on the Web. Having been a working journalist, a journalism educator, a media researcher and finally a news analyst, I felt the need to share what I've learned to help others critically evaluate the enormous variety of what now passes for news as well as other information passed along as factual.

Like most journalists, I consider myself a tough-minded independent. But like most journalists, I lean liberal. I'm convinced that humans depend on each other and need government to brace up the needy and regulate markets so that they work for all. But I also agree with Bill Moyers' analogy: Democracy is like a plane — it requires both a right and left wing. A rational dialogue between liberal and conservative viewpoints yields better results than uniformity on either side.

I could say I remain a practicing Catholic because the nuns know where I live. But it's really because I need all the help I can get. My long-suffering wife is Jewish, however, so I get to enjoy two ancient and beautiful faith traditions. (What's not to like?)

I own no shares of media stock. I'm a penny-ante supporter of the Democratic Party, the American Civil Liberties Union, the Red Cross (making me a bleeding-heart liberal), Doctors without Borders, Amnesty International, CARE, UNICEF, Catholic Charities, the American Jewish World Service, the Union of Concerned Scientists, the Alzheimer's Association, Oxfam, and Bread for the World. In terms of news media, I support my local National Public Radio station, KQED, NPR's On the Media, my local newspaper, the *San Jose Mercury News*, the *New York Times* and occasionally contribute to Democracy Now and FreePress.net. I'm a member of the Association for Education in Journalism and Mass Communication and the National Association for Media Literacy Education. I subscribe to a raft of professional journals and trade publications.

These comprise most of the perception-bending influences on my life. Now, let's explore how to evaluate news and information!

John H. McManus

Sunnyvale, California

May 2012

1

The Age of Transformative Information Paradoxes

Information is as vital to the healthy functioning of communities as clean air...

~ The Knight Commission on the Information Needs of Communities in a Democracy

The infosphere is as necessary to human society as the atmosphere is vital to life on earth.

Without information, even the simplest forms of life wouldn't exist; they depend on information coded on the twisted chains of molecules we call RNA and DNA. And every organism relies on information from within and without to function. The same is true — on a vastly larger scale — for the most complex organisms. Our every thought and action is based on information, and we succeed only to the extent that our information is trustworthy.

Like the atmosphere, the infosphere — all of the public information available to us — is shared. And like the atmosphere, the infosphere is subject to pollution — misinformation. Even if we don't pollute, we all breathe the same air. Whether it's the physical or informational environment, we all share the consequences when it becomes unhealthy.

The Knight Foundation spent a year studying the role of information in society and concluded: "Information is as vital to the healthy functioning of communities as clean air, safe streets, good schools, and public health. People have not typically thought of information this way, but they should."[1]

Just as our atmosphere is changing in ways that affect all of the life that depends on it, our infosphere is undergoing a rapid transformation that is altering how we live and interact. We are entering an age of unprecedented information paradoxes:

- You can look up almost anything on the Internet. But much — perhaps most — of the information offered is really trying to sell you a product, service, or point of view. A Web site aimed at students, **www.martinlutherking.org**, that looks at first like a tribute to the slain civil rights leader is actually a character assassination produced by a white supremacist organization founded by a former Ku Klux Klan leader. A site called **ConsumerNewsReporting.com** mimics *Consumer Reports*, but is really an advertisement featuring a satisfied customer who turns out not to exist.

- New digital technology, especially the Internet, has enabled amateurs to act as journalists, but emptied newsrooms of tens of thousands of trained professionals. With the advertising-sponsored business model of American journalism in tatters, the palaces of the Fourth Estate have become desolate mazes of silent cubicles. Out beyond their grand entrances with their chiseled creed proclaiming journalism necessary for self-government, stretches an uneven, often treacherous, landscape of new content providers eager to claim the unique power of news to define reality.

- With 'round-the-clock cable and 'round-the-world Web sites, we're drowning in news and views, yet parched for relevant, trustworthy reports of current issues and events, especially those closest to home. The signal is becoming lost in the noise.

- The domination of the large metro newspaper has been broken. But those papers, the best of which were trusted referees of political disputes, courts of last resort for the powerless, and honesty-inspiring investigators of public and private fraud, no longer possess the resources — and sometimes the will — to guard or guide their communities. Citizens are now on their own.

- The same technologies that helped the oppressed escape from state propaganda in several Middle East nations during the "Arab Uprising" have eroded the factual common ground that once allowed Americans to conduct civil discussions and reach political consensus. New media gave voice to the voiceless to communicate a narrative of liberation loud enough to topple dictators. They constitute a pillar of freedom. But new cable and Internet media have also empowered competing narratives pitting Democrats against Republicans, liberals versus conservatives, Tea Partiers v. centrists. Each faction can now proclaim not merely its own *opinions*, but its own *facts*. New media are reconstructing the Tower of Babel.

- While the Web spawns diverging versions of truth, it also provides powerful tools for discovering and sharing which claims rest on the strongest evidence. There's a silver lining in the digital cloud.

Comparing the infosphere of the late 20th century to that of the early 21st, resembles holding a child's balloon up to the Goodyear blimp. For those who know how to search and filter it, the explosion of widely available information on the Internet is exciting and empowering. For those who can't distinguish information that's reliable from the rest, it can be bewildering and misleading, a fun house mirror of the world. In a democracy, where the reliably-informed have no greater say in the voting booth than the un- or misinformed, it's essential that a majority learn to discern fact from fiction. Nowhere is this skill more important than in the realm of news — descriptions and interpretations of current issues and events.

From uninvented to invaluable

Since the invention of the World Wide Web in 1990, the Internet has stitched the globe together with threads of copper and optical fiber. In less than two decades it has become an indispensable information utility. By the end of 2010, the Internet hosted more than a quarter billion Web sites. And they are multiplying like sniffles in a children's day care — growing at a rate of almost 60,000 sites per day in 2010.[2] But the Web is a bit like the American West in the 19th century — a vast environment of great variety and interest, but also a place beyond the reach of law where anything goes. Well-compensated publicists cleverly construct a pseudo reality on the Web that serves special interests at the expense of the unwary.[3] For those seeking reliable information, the Web can resemble the legendary maze designed to imprison the Minotaur in confusion as much as it does the Library of Alexandria, said to contain all the written knowledge of the seventh century Mediterranean world.

The Web giveth and the Web taketh away

The Web is by far the most engaging, informative and cost-effective technology journalists have ever possessed — better than TV, magazines and newspapers *combined*. It marries reporting in text to photos and video, allowing each medium to contribute its unique strengths to a multi-media experience. The Web is unencumbered by the delay and enormous cost of printing presses, the need to mash forests into paper, the need to fuel fleets of delivery trucks, and pay paper-flingers. The Web requires no towering, multimillion dollar transmitter nor restrictive government license to operate. It can be carried anywhere in a tablet computer, smart phone or iPod. It turns journalism from a one-way street to a conversational traffic circle. It enables new voices to be heard, rendering obsolete A.J. Liebling's lamentation that "freedom of the press is guaranteed only to those who own one."[4] Web sites also have nearly infinite space for news — breadth *plus* depth — and users can link instantly to other sources and the news organization's own previous coverage, perhaps arranged in an explanatory photo-studded timeline. Not least, mistakes — once made permanent as fast as ink dried on paper — can be corrected as soon as discovered. At long last, journalists possess a news vehicle as awesome as a Ferrari.

But there's little money for gas.

That's because this wondrous technology allows advertisers to drive around the toll booth news media were once able to erect between sellers and buyers. That toll funded large numbers of journalists. It paid the full cost of broadcast news and provided newspapers more than three-quarters of their revenues. Billions of dollars are going, going, gone and not coming back. Advertisers can now reach consumers directly on their own Web sites, on craigslist, or with the help of search companies like Google. No longer must advertisers purchase the attention of a hundred pairs of eyeballs to find one potential customer. As empowering as the Web has been for journalists, it's been even more of a god-send to advertisers.

The rise of the amateurs and fall of the pros

The dollar drain is sucking staff from newspaper, broadcast, and magazine newsrooms.[5] Into the vacuum left by the departing reporters and editors — usually starting with the most experienced (and therefore best paid) — surges a Mardi Gras parade of Twittering texters, Flik'ring photographers, bloviating bloggers, and YouTubing videographers. There are high-minded — but usually under-trained and under-funded — citizen journalists.[6] There are advocates of every spot and stripe, corporate and government publicists, and advertisers by the gigabyte. All doing, or pretending to do, news.

But few of these new providers and commentators are aware of, much less constrained by, the ethical codes of journalism.[7] Few enjoy the resources and insulation from conflicts of interest that professional newsrooms once afforded. They are no substitute for the journalists who have been displaced.[8]

> "You have this incredible moment of abundance. There are more stories; there are more media outlets. [But] we're actually experiencing really serious shortages of a certain type of reporting, which we call local accountability reporting..."[9]
>
> ~ Steven Waldman, author of the Federal Communication Commission's 2011 study, "The information needs of communities"

Many of the new news outlets don't even disclose who they are, much less who pays the piper for their tunes. And what's left of the traditional media too often substitute sensation for substance and stenography for shoe-leather.[10] Almost all are cutting corners, especially the corners where investigative reporters once sat. The result is a surfeit of news and information from providers of uncertain reliability coupled with a scarcity of reporting and commentary from trusted brands. This is particularly true at the city and metropolitan level where newspapers that once slammed on front porches now flutter.[11]

> "You have no one covering the agencies anymore and that's true not just in the federal government, but in the state and city governments."[12]
>
> ~ Ken Auletta, author and media writer for *The New Yorker*

The rise of competing narratives, the loss of common ground

In 2011, subjugated masses in Tunisia, Egypt, Libya and elsewhere used new media to stimulate and organize protests against established dictators. Social networks like Facebook and Twitter allowed people to share an alternative description of events free of government control. That narrative featured satellite- and Internet-borne images from Al Jazeera, documentation of their autocratic leaders' corruption on WikiLeaks, and thousands of images from cell phone cameras.[13] More credible than official propaganda, it electrified a population aggrieved by joblessness, government corruption and rising food prices and urged them into the streets to demand democratic change. Thousands of separate sparks of outrage were suddenly connected into a jolting current of change.

But, like a sword that can be used both to defend and attack, new communication technologies can divide as well as unite. They allow factions on the political left and right to construct alternate versions of news and information. Nowhere is this more apparent than in political campaigns. "Across the years we've increasingly moved to a kind of campaign structure that makes it harder to thoughtfully consider alternatives," noted University of Pennsylvania media analyst Kathleen Hall Jamieson. "We've got to find a way to fix this. We're at a very, very critical time right now."[14]

"It's increasingly possible to live in an online world in which you do have your own facts."[15]

~ Eli Pariser, author of *The Filter Bubble*

Americans are rapidly losing the informational commons, the town square, of the late 20th Century. Then nearly everyone in the community read the same metro newspaper, and watched national newscasts anchored by Dan Rather, Peter Jennings or Tom Brokaw, all of which were informed by the same principles of journalism. Our opinions surely clashed then, but less often our facts. For better and for worse, that scarcity of news sources has given way to so much abundance that we're all now our own news gatekeepers.

For the first time in history, we can fashion our own news diet, not some neutral editor. If we wish, we can tailor the news to our own biases and share no common ground for discussion with fellow citizens on the issues of the day. In fact, Eli Pariser, former executive director of the liberal lobbying organization, Move-on.org, contends that search engines such as Google have installed algorithms that personalize our information searches based on our past preferences.[16] Without our knowing it, our informational horizons can be narrowed.

But most of us *prefer* to live in segregated information neighborhoods. Summarizing research in psychology, Cordelia Fine of the Melbourne Business School wrote, "We humans quickly develop an irrational loyalty to our beliefs, and work hard to find evidence that supports those opinions and to discredit, discount or avoid information that does not."[17] That has contributed to partisan gridlock in our politics, an inability to confront the important domestic and international challenges of the day. As *New York Times* business columnist Joe Nocera pointed out, "in Washington these days, there is no such thing as bipartisan. On every major issue facing the country, Democrats and Republicans have competing narratives."[18]

In terms of how many will be affected and how adversely, no problem we face surpasses global climate change with its prospect of ankle-deep coastal cities, salad-bowl farming regions desiccating to dust bowls, super storms and floods spawned by the greater capacity of a warmer atmosphere to carry moisture, and oceans absorbing heat and becoming more acidic faster than fish and plants can adapt. Perhaps because its impact is so vast, no issue is more subject to "competing narratives." Type the phrase "global climate change" into

Google News and you'll see almost 2 million articles, framing the issue from every point on the compass. The volume alone can be overwhelming, like trying to drink from a fire hose.

> "Man-made global warming is a hoax. Global warming is a hoax."[19]
>
> ~ Rush Limbaugh
>
> *vs.*
>
> "The earth is warming and human activity is the primary cause."[20]
>
> ~ Union of Concerned Scientists

Drawing on parallel but polarized universes of news and comment, Americans have become less able to plot a safe course than a squirrel in traffic. Astonishingly, as the scientific evidence for global warming solidifies, the political will to avert catastrophe is dissolving. Surveys show fewer Americans believed the consensus of climate scientists in 2010 than did in 2006. With no common ground, Republicans and Democrats can't agree on what's real.[21]

The silver lining

There is a bright silver lining, however, in the digital cloud. If you know how to use them, tools such as Google advanced search, social media such as Facebook and Web sites like FactCheck.org, PolitiFact.com, Snopes.com, NewsTrust.net, CNN's "Keeping them honest," and the *Washington Post's* "Fact Checker" can help you separate the signal from the noise. We've never before had such powerful help in vetting truth claims. And, if you're willing to open your mind wide enough to recognize your own biases (everybody's got 'em), this little book can help you develop your own BS (**B**ald **S**ophistry) detector. That's important because what James Madison wrote with a goose quill in 1822 is as true as if it were Tweeted today:

> Knowledge will forever govern ignorance, and a people who mean to be their own governors, must arm themselves with the power knowledge gives.[22]

What's at stake

Of all knowledge, news is arguably the most important. That's because we act, not on reality, but on whatever we take to be true at the time. People have always organized their lives by what they thought was true. If they believed a certain dance brought rain, they danced when it was dry. If sacrificing animals or humans were believed to placate the gods, then such creatures were ritually killed. If we believe higher education is the key to a financially secure future, we flock to college.

While Madison was president, on the day before Christmas 1814, the young American republic signed the Treaty of Ghent with Great Britain officially ending the War of 1812. Fifteen days later and 3,000 miles away across the Atlantic, British Major-General Edward Pakenham ordered a dawn assault by 11,000 sailors and Red Coats at muddy Chalmette Plantation, just outside of New Orleans. By nightfall 2,042 of the British were dead, wounded or missing, along with 71 Americans. Sir Edward did not survive long enough to learn that the war was over before the battle began.[23]

The Battle of New Orleans was fought before news spread faster than wind could push sails or horses could carry mail bags. Today news rides radio waves bouncing off satellites at the speed of light. But the principle that people act on what they *think* is real, not on what *is* real, is timeless.

On March 20, 2003, the Americans and British launched a predawn assault on Saddam Hussein's desert fortifications, thinking that the Iraqis possessed "weapons of mass destruction" that were aimed at America and its allies. The Anglo-American case for war included charges that Saddam helped sponsor the terror attacks on Manhattan and the Pentagon on Sept. 11, 2001. Neither rationale reflected reality, but tens — by some estimates hundreds — of thousands of Iraqis died along with almost 5,000 American and British soldiers in a war and ensuing insurgency that would last eight more years. When the full costs of the war and taking care of injured soldiers, some for a lifetime, are totaled, a Nobel Prize-winning economist estimates our bill will exceed three trillion taxpayer dollars.[24] (That's enough to buy a 2010 Mercedes C Class luxury sedan for every American between the ages of 18 and 40).

"The future of our self-government, the future of our democracy hinges on having an informed electorate, an electorate with sufficient depth and breadth of information that they can make sense out of all of the complex problems that we face and make intelligent decisions for the future of the country."[25]

Former Federal Communications Commission member Michael J. Copps

Regardless of why it's unreliable, once acted upon, the effect of bad information is the same: We make decisions based on a pseudo-reality, a false consciousness. To the extent that we are misled, our decisions can lead us to grief individually and as a nation.

At the personal level, bad information may take the form of a bum investment tip from a supposed insider, or a Web site describing the latest medical "miracle." Or a real estate column urging year-in-year-out that "it's the perfect time to buy a house." Such advice helped inflate a bubble in housing prices that, when it burst, submerged millions of homes into debt higher than their value.

For personal decisions affecting just ourselves or our families, critical thinking about information can minimize harm. We can recognize most fraud and misguided advice. But in a democracy, bad information can wreak havoc even when many people recognize its flaws. The majority rules, no matter how misinformed. That's why vetting news and information should be a social activity shared with others. As we'll see in the final chapter, new social media make this easy to do.

Reliable news is more valuable than ever

News describes and explains change. By definition, its principal concern is what's *new*. Its value rises as technologies of every sort are pushing shockwaves of change through our society at an accelerating pace.

Just as a classroom globe that still maps the Soviet Union or the assumption that the world's climate remains stable over a lifetime is outdated, the expiration date on almost everything we know is becoming shorter. Old news. Not just in politics, science, and technology, but in medicine, education, agriculture, retail, transportation, energy, even how and where we work and what we're paid. We live in an information age on steroids.

Whether it arrives by sail or satellite, on paper, television, computer screen, smart phone or over the back fence, news matters. It's worth considerable effort to avoid being fooled. As National Public Radio media critic Brooke Gladstone recently put it: "The responsibility is now on the news consumer. This is a *caveat emptor* world. Let the buyer beware."[26]

What's in the book

Any exploration of bias must begin with an examination of the slippery nature of truth. Next we'll look at where bias comes from, at two levels: the personal, and within the institutions that provide most of our news and information. Then we'll reconnoiter a more realistic standard for judging such information than the impossible and, I will argue, undesirable notion of objectivity. Next, we'll see how a simple test for reliability — the SMELL test — can help us avoid being fooled, both personally as consumers, and collectively as citizens. Because media are becoming more visually oriented, there's a chapter devoted to visual literacy — how to detect and avoid manipulation through photos and videos. The penultimate chapter analyzes the most common traps of the deception trade and how to sidestep them. Finally, we'll explore new ways to avoid being fooled — and fooling ourselves — using the Internet to its full capacity.

2

Truth vs. Truthiness

The truth shall set you free.

~ Jesus of Nazareth (John 8:32)

Jesus, in the Christian bible, says truth leads to liberty. But Stephen, in the "Colbert Report," says truth is obsolete; the new standard is "truthiness." This chapter explores three propositions about the nature of truth in an age of truthiness:

1. **What we call truth is really a simulation or virtual reality.**

2. **While we can amplify our senses with technology, we can never be sure that the virtual reality within our heads matches what's outside.**

3. **We may think we are in charge of assigning meaning to what we see and hear, but most of our sense-making is programmed by others.**

As a self-professed fake journalist, Stephen Colbert mocks the concept of truth. He describes truthiness as a feeling of confidence that something is true that is liberated from any thinking of one's own or reference to others' thinking, such as might

Courtesy of Thisdayinquotes.com

appear in an "elitist" medium, like a book. Truth is for those who "think with their heads," Colbert deadpans. "Truthiness" is for "those who *know* with their hearts."[1]

At the heart of Colbert's humor lies the incongruity of someone dressed in the authority of a dark suit speaking complete nonsense with absolute conviction. But the joke is on us. We've all seen and heard more than enough guys and gals like that at work, in the marketplace, and in politics. They are frequently in error, but rarely in doubt.

In April 2011, for example, Senate Republican Whip John Kyl set a personal best for truthiness when he claimed in a debate about federal abortion funding: "If you want an abortion, you go to Planned Parenthood, and that's well over 90 percent of what Planned Parenthood does."[2] After others confronted him with the correct figure, about 3 percent, Sen. Kyl's office replied that the claim "was not intended to be a factual statement." If a senator giving a speech on an important national issue in the U.S. Capitol does not even *intend* to speak factually, truthiness has become more than a gag on Comedy Central. It's become a weapon of mass deception.

Philosophers have long disputed the nature of truth. While those debates are beyond the scope of this book, the concept of truth lies at the very center of our search for reliable news and information. So it's essential to examine it, if only to discover that it differs from what many of us were taught — that truth is self-evident and unchanging.

Perhaps the most common definition of truth is this: a faithful account of what's real. Sounds simple. However it's anything but, as we shall see below.

1. What we call truth is really a simulation or virtual reality

The only way we can know it comes through our five senses and our brain, which interprets those electrochemical neural impulses from our eyes, ears, nose, tongue, and skin. But our senses are only capable of receiving a sliver of what the universe has to offer. Visible light comprises only a narrow range of the frequencies of radiant energy, about 2.5%.[3] Similarly, our ears miss tones above and below a thin band of pitches. (Your dog can do better!) Our tongues can only identify five basic tastes. Our skin can sense a traveling ant but not a mite, much less the presence of a germ.

Not only do our senses miss most of what's going on around us, they transform what they do receive. Electromagnetic radiation oscillating at one frequency we call blue, at another, red. A drum makes no sound, only waves of air pressure, until it beats against the tympanum in our ear. Cognitive scientist Robert Ornstein points out:

> The world outside is silent, dull. It could be called odorless, colorless, and tasteless, for there is no color in nature, no sound, no touch, no smell. All these wonders exist inside the shell that the mind creates for us to live in. Out of the few forlorn signals that get inside, we create an entire world in the same way as do architects who create whole buildings using only lines on paper.[4]

Even though our senses miss most of what's going on, they still produce more data than our brains can handle. So our brains have been shaped by evolution to filter out most of this information so they can concentrate on those sensory signals most vital to survival. They are, for example, more attuned to motion than stillness — to the leaping tiger rather than the tree. We notice loud noises more than the background. We are more aware of pain than comfort and more sensitive to loss than gain. We pay greater attention to change than sameness.[5]

Psychologists say we have evolved with two, almost opposite, ways of thinking. Most of the time, we operate in an *automatic* mode: quickly, intuitively, and effortlessly. We're not even aware of it, like how to ride a bike once you've learned. Automatic mode allows us to cope with danger, as well as life's complexity and pace, without conscious effort. But we are easily fooled in automatic mode because we jump to conclusions based on associations rather than logic. If we subconsciously connect pizza with comfort, we may eat it without bothering to consider whether it's healthy. Only rarely do we engage our brains in the *reflective* mode, the second type of thinking. Reflection requires conscious effort. It's slow. But because we reason deductively from principles we've learned over time, the results are more trustworthy. Both types of thinking are influenced by our experiences — particularly the most recent and emotional — and our knowledge and beliefs, as well as our purpose at the time.

These limits on our ability to interpret reality should create gradations in what we take to be true. Our most reliable path toward truth arises from reflective thinking. When conducted with others, it's called the empirical method. This is the approach taken by science and to a lesser degree by courts of law. It's a description of reality based on the logical construction of evidence from independent observations that has survived efforts to prove it false.

But we take many things to be true that have not endured so rigorous a test. Most things, in fact. We might accept as true what a Web site, a TV show, a book, a parent or other authority tells us, what our friends or peers say, or just a rumor. We often draw conclusions from a few haphazard observations. Indeed, some of what we consider true cannot even be subjected to an empirical analysis — notions of God and religion, for example.

2. While we can amplify our senses with technology, we can never be sure that the virtual reality within our heads matches what's outside

Because empirical truth is a *description* of reality, it's a human product. It can be written as words or an equation, but either way it's a human invention. Its value is based on how useful it is to help us cope with the world around us.

We've had the most success describing reality when we've relied on the scientific method. That involves careful *observation* by more than one person and the application of *logic* to make sense of what we observe. Science looks for patterns in nature that have a high probability of occurring. Generalizations about these patterns become laws when they have survived enough tests of their validity raised by competing theories.

Science has expanded our ability to sense the world with telescopes, X-rays, and other wonderful instruments. But we still "see" the universe incompletely. As technology has enhanced our senses, some of what we once believed to be true has changed. The first century CE (common era) Egyptian astronomer Claudius Ptolemy's interpretation of the cosmos got the roundness of the earth right but portrayed it as the center of the cosmos, circled by the moon, Mercury, Venus, the sun, Mars, Jupiter, and Saturn.

A thousand years ago, everybody "knew" that the sun orbited the Earth. You only had to look to the east in the morning to see the sun rise and track it across the sky until it set in the western sky to "prove" it. Of course, we didn't know then that the Earth was spinning, making the sun only appear to travel across the sky. Most also didn't know that the Earth was round (or as we've learned more recently, slightly ovoid). It seemed so obviously flat.

The truths of those days were in people's heads and bore little relation to the physical universe. As we learned more through the development of better tools — telescopes and ships that could sail around the Earth — what everyone accepted as true became false, even silly.

But even science can't guarantee correspondence with reality. The facts about the physical universe keep changing. The atom ain't what it used to be. Until the turn of the 20th century, it was thought to be the smallest building block of nature. In the virtual reality our minds construct, that's how we "saw" it. Then we discovered electrons, and later neutrons and protons. More recently, we've learned of smaller particles — six "flavors" of quarks, and leptons.[6] As I write, the search for the Higgs boson is underway at the Large Hadron Collider under the Franco-Swiss border.

"If you look at the history of science, you'll see that almost every belief that at some point has been proclaimed the truth about the world has at some later point be revealed to be absolutely false. That is, in fact, how science moves forward."[7]

~ Kathryn Schultz, author of *Being Wrong: Adventures in the Margin of Error*

Chastened by new discoveries, scientists consider all knowledge about nature to be tentative – the best we can do right now. We never know what's just around the learning corner that will rewrite our notions of truth.

But just because our best claims of truth are uncertain and subject to change, that doesn't mean they don't matter or shouldn't guide us. We have made great strides in our ability to flourish as a species by following the best knowledge of the day. It's allowed us to make barren deserts flower and fruit, to routinely travel at nearly the speed of sound, to eliminate diseases that crippled our grandparents, to expand our lifespan, and to squeeze thousands of bands — even orchestras — into our iPods!

3. We may think we are in charge of assigning meaning to what we see and hear, but most of our sense-making is programmed by others

Because of slight physical differences in our eyes, ears, taste buds, and other sensory organs, we don't all experience the world the same way. And the neurochemical signals traveling from our senses to our brains are interpreted in light of our unique experiences. So some of what we take to be true is unique to us, perhaps stemming from a religious or other deeply-felt experience or an idiosyncratic set of beliefs. Nevertheless, most of what we accept as true or factual is based on a description of reality that *others* agree is true. We are programmed by the culture of our place and time.

Even what we experience directly, we usually interpret as we have been taught. For thousands of years men have experienced firsthand the intelligence, courage, and wisdom of women. But until very recently in human history, it appears that most men considered women inferior. Not capable of voting in the U.S. until 1920. Not worthy of a university education until late in the 19th Century. Not accepted as rabbis, ministers, or mullahs until very recently. Still not welcome to become Catholic priests. In Saudi Arabia, not yet trusted to drive a car!

Try this thought experiment: You attend a party where the host serves a deep-fried, breaded finger food that looks something like an onion ring. You taste one and find it's delicious. "What is it?" you ask. "Deep-fried worms," the host replies. Would you lose your appetite?[8]

If so, notice that your own judgment of a pleasant taste was overruled by what you had been taught about eating worms. And the discovery that you were chewing on worms affected you not just intellectually — "Oh, that's interesting" — but as a visceral rejection (maybe even ejection). *Escargot* anyone?

The ideas about what's true exist in our heads, but they are powerfully influenced by others. In most ancient tribal societies, shamans and elders held the authority to say what was true and what was false. Later, religious authorities, kings, queens, and the nobility would claim it. In our day, teachers, scientists, political and religious leaders, and news media are the most powerful truth-tellers, at least in developed nations.

Oral, and later written, myths enabled accepted interpretations of basic questions about truth — the nature of humans, the Earth and cosmos, God or gods, order, virtue and vice — to spread through a tribe or a people. *The Iliad, The Odyssey,* the Hebrew and Christian Bibles, and the Bhagavad-Gita ("Song of God" in Sanskrit) are ancient examples of this. The Declaration of Independence, the U.S. Constitution and the United Nations' Universal Declaration of Human Rights are more recent ones.

Culture comprises all of the stories we tell about ourselves and our environment, in whatever medium. Those stories are grounded in shared myths and beliefs as well as the wisdom and knowledge available at a given place and time. Because so little of what we take as truth arises from empirical investigation, we rely on culture as a social binding agent. It allows our individual reality simulations to sync enough for us to get along within our community. But culture can also be a blinding agent when the cultures of different communities clash. Each community believes its interpretation corresponds to reality, so the other must be in error. As we'll see in the next chapter, even within a single nation there are subcultures which chafe against each other. The misperceptions engendered by those cultural differences breed bias.

3

Where Bias Comes From

Why can't they produce a fair, balanced, objective and non-partisan newspaper – that reflects my point of view?

~ Classic cartoon caption

We all like to think we see the world just as it is. Those who disagree with us are misinformed, mischievous, morally-challenged or missing a screw. But — alas! — we are all subject to bias. That's because rather than investigating the world empirically, most of the time we rely for our sense of reality on others who are like us. Like a flying wedge of geese in the autumn sky, it takes much less effort to follow in formation than set out alone.

Just as similar types of birds flock together, we form subcultures, even within one society. From the inside looking out, the lens of culture looks perfectly clear. We don't notice our own group's biases because they are taken-for-granted. But when our views differ from another group's perspective, the "distortions" in *their* cultural lenses are glaringly obvious. "Be reasonable!" we naively plead, "see it my way."

The Christian scriptures quote Jesus telling his disciples, "First take the log out of your own eye, and then you will see clearly to take the speck out of your brother's eye" (Matthew 7:5). It's excellent advice for everyone. When we look for bias in how journalists and other information sources perceive and describe the world, we must also examine *our own* prejudices. Otherwise, we're likely to fall into the cynic's trap of seeing bias in any description or interpretation of reality with which we disagree. As Jesus observed, bias is not something added on to a crystalline perception, it shapes the very act of seeing.

This chapter explores six propositions about our ability to see reality clearly:

1. **Even when we watch the same thing, we don't see the same thing.**

2. **We forget that what we see depends on where we are observing from and when; we treat snapshots as if they were panoramic videos.**

3. **Rather than seeing everything before us, we focus on only a part of it.**

4. **We don't just record what's in focus like a camera; as dot-connecting animals, we unconsciously select just a fraction of what's in focus and impose meaning.**

5. **We are more likely to notice what confirms our expectations than what contradicts them.**

6. **Bias begins with self-interest, but there are other equally subconscious and predictable layers based on race, class, geography, gender, generation, and other cultural groupings.**

Perhaps the best-known study of the perceptual origins of bias was conducted in the fall of 1951 and based on, of all things, a football game: Princeton vs. Dartmouth. From all accounts it was a vicious game. In the second quarter Princeton's All-American quarterback, Dick Kazmaier, left the game with a broken nose. One quarter later a Dartmouth player's leg was broken. Heated words and penalty flags flew back and forth.[1]

After the game, student newspapers on both campuses erupted in outrage.

The *Daily Princetonian* charged: "This observer has never seen quite such a disgusting exhibition of so-called 'sport.' Both teams were guilty, but the blame must be laid primarily on Dartmouth's doorstep." It went on to accuse Dartmouth of "a deliberate attempt to cripple Dick Kazmaier."

The student editors of the *Dartmouth* scoffed: "Kazmaier was the star, an All-American. Other stars have been injured before, but Kazmaier had been built to represent a Princeton idol. When an idol is hurt there is only one recourse — the tag of dirty football." They went on to accuse Princeton's coach of ordering his players to take revenge on Dartmouth's team.

1. Even when we watch the same thing, we don't see the same thing

The viewpoints on each campus diverged so widely that a professor at each school agreed to conduct an experiment. They took a film of the game and showed it to students at both universities. As students watched the identical film, they were asked to fill in a questionnaire counting the number of rule violations they saw each team commit and characterize each as "mild" or "flagrant."

Although the game took place in broad daylight, following rules of football accepted by both sides and enforced by referees, and both groups of (smart?) Ivy League students saw the same action onscreen, the Dartmouth and Princeton students marked their questionnaires very differently. On average, Dartmouth students allocated rule violations evenly between the two teams, while Princeton students "saw" more than twice as many violations by Dartmouth gridders as

Princeton players. Each side also regarded the other team's violations as more serious than its own squad's.

The professors concluded that "the 'game' actually was many different games and that each version of the events that transpired was just as 'real' to a particular person as other versions were to other people."[2] In other words, the truth about what happened differed somewhat for each observer. But those observers loyal to Dartmouth green clustered around a different truth than those partial to Princeton orange. The lesson? Our allegiances and associations affect what we see. Notice that this flips the conventional wisdom — "seeing is believing" — on its head. For most of those watching the game film, *believing (in one side or the other) was seeing.*

2. We forget that what we see depends on where we are observing from and when; we treat snapshots as if they were panoramic videos

It may seem too obvious to mention, but the fact that we observe from a particular place at a particular time limits our grasp of the whole truth. Our vantage point might not be the best place to see what's going on. And our timing might be off, arriving too early or — as is usually the case with journalists — too late to observe something for ourselves. When that happens, we all rely on sources. But each of those sources suffers the same limitation of a fixed viewpoint at a given time. It's a profound problem for journalism.

Former NBC and MSNBC reporter Ashleigh Banfield explained the limitations of viewpoint experienced by reporters, such as her, who were embedded with American soldiers firing at Saddam Hussein's army in 2003. The coverage, she explained, "certainly did show the American side of things, because that's where we were shooting [video] from." But, she continued:

> You didn't see where those bullets landed. You didn't see what happened when the mortar

landed. A puff of smoke is not what a mortar looks like when it explodes, believe me. There are horrors that were completely left out of this war. ...

... There is a grand difference between journalism and coverage, and getting access does not mean you're getting the story; it just means you're getting one more arm or leg of the story. And that's what we got, and it was a glorious, wonderful picture that had a lot of people watching and a lot of advertisers excited about cable news. But it wasn't journalism.... We got rid of a dictator, we got rid of a monster, but we didn't see what it took to do that.[3]

Ms. Banfield's candor is uncommon in journalism. Executives don't like to reveal how one-sided and time-bound many news reports are.

So three questions we should ask about anyone's description of an event are: *Where were they or their sources watching from? And when? Were they in a position to know what they claim to know? What couldn't they notice from their vantage point?*

3. Rather than seeing everything before us, we focus on only a part

Even if we're limited to observing from one spot at any given moment, our five senses take in a great deal of information. More than our brains can handle.[4] So we're forced to focus on a few things rather than the whole panorama.

Test this the next time you're in a group of people, perhaps a meeting, class or religious service. Depending on where you're sitting, within the "screen" of your vision, you may be able to see many people. They may differ from one another in.

Image from Wikimedia Commons

multiple ways: gender, race, ethnicity, body size and shape, clothing, and posture But I'll bet you can't describe the characteristics of each person until you place him/er at the center of your vision. Our vision resembles the focal point of a camera. Our subject is sharply focused, while objects closer and farther away are blurred.

Our other senses are similarly focused. The person who convened the gathering might be speaking loudly, but we can reduce the noise to an incoherent drone as we listen to a friend whisper from the next seat. We notice foods smells more before dinner than afterwards. We can eat a sandwich and barely taste it when we're absorbed in a conversation or reading something.

We can even turn off our senses and go inside to our imagination or memory. We might replay a compliment or complaint from a boss or friend, or a passionate moment. And if none of these happened, we can imagine how it would (or should!) have happened. We can be lost in our thoughts and not see or hear the speaker at all. (As a professor I've stared out at glassy eyes that were pointed my way. But I was only seeing the backs of screens playing an internal movie more compelling than my words.)

Our attention is not like a mirror, capturing everything happening before it. It's more like the narrow beam of a flashlight in the dark, illuminating particular parts of our external environment or the internal landscape of our minds.

So two more questions to ponder are: *What were we or our information-provider paying the most attention to? What might have been missed?*

4. We don't just record what's in focus like a camera; as dot-connecting animals we unconsciously select just a fraction of what's in focus and impose meaning

Even when we turn the searchlight of our attention on someone or something, we don't record it the way a camera might. We perceive *selectively* and *imaginatively*. Humans tend to organize the data their senses feed them into patterns. We are dot-connecting animals. Where there is no logical order, we often make one up.

Ancient people would behold a sky bright with stars and "see" a big dipper, a hunter, a bull, a scorpion, or a cross. Believers see the face of a saint in the bark pattern of a tree. When looking at an ink blot, we might see demons or lovers. This happens below the level of our conscious awareness in our automatic thinking mode. If I type a colon then a dash followed by a right parenthesis, you are likely to rotate these three keystrokes 90 degrees, assemble them into a single symbol, and infer ☺ from :-).

The ability to connect dots has obvious evolutionary value. Making connections among pieces of sensory information helped early humans cope with a dangerous environment. Thanks to our automatic mode of thinking, when we experience something, our minds don't dispassionately assemble the data from our eyes, ears, and nose, then logically evaluate it and render a judgment about the reality we face. That would have taken too long to avoid a tribal warrior's hurled spear. We're wired to create a pattern that we can act on in the blink of an eye.

As Malcolm Gladwell described in his book *Blink*, these instant, intuitive patterns remain very helpful. They might alert us to danger by picking up an expression on the face of someone about to attack us. They might cue us to romantic possibilities when we sense someone likes us. They can alert us to fraud when we sense something isn't quite right.

Mr. Gladwell quoted police officers, soldiers, and athletes describing the positive aspects of selective perception. It filters out irrelevant information and sharpens our focus on what we are doing so effectively that time may seem to slow down. He offered this description of a policeman and his partner facing a gunman:

> When he started toward us, it was almost like it was in slow motion and everything went into a tight focus. ... My vision focused on his torso and the gun. I couldn't tell you what his left hand was doing. I have no idea. I didn't hear a thing, not one thing. Alan [his partner] had fired one round when I shot my first pair, but I didn't hear him shoot.[5]

5. We are more likely to notice what confirms our expectations than what contradicts them

The selective and imaginative perception of our automatic system of thinking can also get us into trouble. It has at least two known and related biases. First, *it imposes a pattern that's known and familiar on the unknown and unfamiliar.* Second, *it provides a picture more likely to confirm our beliefs (including our prejudices) than to contradict them.*

Experiments have shown that we are more likely to perceive what's familiar to us than what's unfamiliar.[6] So we tend to see something new not as it is, but in terms of something more familiar. When the steam locomotive was new, we called it the "iron horse." The first automobile was a "horseless carriage." The early radio was called a "wireless," because it could send Morse code without telegraph wire. The Internet was introduced as an "information superhighway."

Psychologists say we also notice things that *support* our beliefs more than those that *contradict* them.[7] This is called "confirmatory bias." If we think someone dislikes us, we might notice the person passing on a crowded walkway and perceive a lack of a glance in our direction as a deliberate snub. The person, however, might simply not have seen us. Conversely, if we think someone likes us, we might see a nod under similar circumstances as confirming our belief, even if the nod signals no more than recognition.

Stereotypes often shape these selective perceptions. If we think women are poorer drivers than men, we notice the woman standing beside the wrecked vehicle on the side of the road, but ignore the man in similar circumstances. If we think Jews are more likely to be swindlers than Christians, we take Bernard Madoff's conviction as proof, but overlook scams perpetrated by Catholics and Protestants. (Charles Ponzi, after whom schemes like Mr. Madoff's are named, was a Roman Catholic born in Italy.)

This is why stereotypes are so dangerous. They can cause us to misjudge others without even being aware of it. So we can add to our questions about our own and other's accounts: *Does it stereotype or discount by race, religion or other type? Whose viewpoints are privileged and whose are marginalized or missing?*

6. Bias begins with self-interest, but there are other equally subconscious and predictable layers based on race, class, geography, gender, generation, and other cultural groupings

We have no choice but to make sense of the world from within our own skulls. We are always most aware of our own experience, our own pains and pleasures, our own needs, wants and fears. Evolution has formed us to see the world not as it is, but as it *relates to us*, especially how it might serve or threaten our interests. To survive in a competitive environment humans have had to look out for themselves and their tribe. We are inherently self-interested. This is where bias begins.

Unless we are as empathetic as a Gandhi or Martin Luther King Jr., our concern for, and knowledge of, others falls off rapidly with distance from our own interests. Loving our neighbors as ourselves is a wonderful goal, but almost impossible to achieve. (As for loving strangers, much less our enemies — God help us!)

Our preoccupation with ourselves and those close to us explains why Princeton students saw their varsity classmates performing differently than did Dartmouth students. That's why we identify more easily with those of similar race, class, gender, generation, neighborhood, nationality, religion, or profession and than those who differ from us. It's why men have to be trained to lower the toilet seat. (Where you stand depends on whether you stand or sit!) In addition to misunderstanding, otherness breeds apathy, if not contempt. (What's so difficult about putting the damn seat down?!!)

Don't get me wrong. Self-reliance is a virtue. Though no one can manage it alone, we need to take care of and love ourselves. Moderate self-interest is healthy. But it becomes corrosive when what we do for ourselves harms others. Selfishness is a vice — one we hate to admit.

To maintain our self-esteem even when we are serving our self-interest at others' expense, humans engage in what researchers call "motivated blindness." It's "the tendency to overlook information that works against one's best interest," according to Max H. Bazerman, a professor of business administration at Harvard and Ann E. Tenbrunsel, a professor of management at Notre Dame. They conclude: "Ample research shows that people who have a vested self-interest, even the most honest among us, have difficulty being objective. Worse yet, they fail to recognize their lack of objectivity."[8]

To avoid being fooled, we should examine the predictable, but invisible-to-us, layers of social bias that radiate from our self-interest.

Social fault lines: Predictable biases in American culture

The late Robert C. Maynard, one of the first African-American reporters at the *Washington Post* and later publisher of the *Oakland Tribune,* had an insight late in his career. The San Francisco Bay Area, where the *Tribune* is located, has a number of earthquake faults. So does society, Mr. Maynard recognized. We are divided, he realized, by subcultures based on race, class, geography, gender, and generation. Much of our misunderstanding of each other, he wrote, arises from these "fault lines." When we peer across one of these fault lines, we might misconstrue what we see because the terrain is not as familiar as it is within our own race, class, neighborhood, gender, and generation. Or because we've been led to believe certain things about other people and places.[9]

As new media allow us to choose both our facts and opinions, and as we live, work and associate with others like us, these fault lines grow from cracks to chasms. University of Virginia social psychologist Jonathan Haidt observed:

America has ... become in the post-war world gradually a nation of lifestyle enclaves where people choose to self-segregate. If people are concentrating just where people are like them, then they're not exposed to ideas from the other side from people they can actually like and respect. If you get all your ideas about the other side from the Internet, where there's no human connection, it's just so easy and automatic to reject it and demonize it. So once we've sorted ourselves into homogeneous moral communities, it becomes a lot harder to work together.[10]

The fault line of race

The public reaction to the acquittal of O.J. Simpson in 1995 revealed this tear in our social fabric. After a televised, year-long trial and almost obsessive news coverage, the Hall-of-Fame running back was judged not guilty of slashing the throats of his estranged wife and her companion. Two weeks after the Oct. 3 verdict, the Gallup Poll found that 89% of black respondents agreed that the jury had made the "right decision," against only 36% of whites.[11]

Reacting to polar differences in the televised reaction to the verdict between blacks and whites, *New York Times* columnist Anthony Lewis wrote: "We knew we were a divided society. But not before had the depth of that division been so instantly dramatized. It was as if we lived in different countries."[12]

You might think journalists would exhibit a milder version of these divisions; they're always proclaiming themselves "objective," or "fair and balanced." But on the tenth anniversary of the Simpson verdict, NPR's Karen Grigsby Bates asked journalists to recall the day the trial ended:

Judy Muller was in ABC's Los Angeles bureau watching TV monitors as she waited to write a piece on the Simpson verdict that would run on "Nightline." When the verdict was read, Ms. Muller, who is white, remembers that her jaw dropped. "I think the reaction in the newsroom was the same as newsrooms and cafes and diners all across the country. I think the reaction split down racial lines." Other journalists Ms. Bates interviewed responded similarly.[13]

We can now ask the following questions: *Is our viewpoint, or the information-provider's, biased by race? Do they quote sources presenting racially and ethnically diverse perspectives? Which viewpoints are marginalized or missing?*

The fault line of class

Have you ever heard someone say, "If you're so damn smart, why aren't you rich?" The saying reflects an article of faith: We Americans tend to believe we live in a classless meritocracy, a country where everyone with talent who makes an effort can land a good job and salary. From this perspective, either the poor lack talent or they are lazy — or both. Any way you slice it, they are seen as inferior to the well-to-do.

But sociologists can provide lots of statistics showing that the American playing field is not level. The differences in outcomes — such as lifetime accumulation of wealth — can be reliably predicted from differences in inputs, for example, the resources a family can provide for its children.[14] It was, but should not have been, surprising that the Pew Charitable Trust's Economic Mobility Project found Americans are less socially mobile from one generation to the next than Canadians and the citizens of every European nation in the study.[15] We are blind to class bias, yet it alters our perceptions as surely as a magnet bends a line of iron filings.

Sociologists William Thompson and Joseph Hickey wrote:

> It is impossible to understand people's behavior ... without the concept of social stratification, because class position has a pervasive influence on almost everything ... the clothes we wear ... the television shows we watch ... the colors we paint our homes in and the names we give our pets. ... Our position in the social hierarchy affects our health, happiness, and even how long we will live.[16]

We can now ask the following questions: *Is our viewpoint, or the information-provider's, biased by class? Are there sources presenting different class perspectives? Which viewpoints are marginalized or missing?*

The fault line of geography

The fault line of geography concerns the physical location — neighborhood, region of the country, nation — where we grew up or have lived most of our lives. People who grew up on farms differ in outlook from those who grew up in suburbs, who differ from those who grew up in the city. Some in "red" states would like to secede from "blue" states and some in "blue" states wouldn't mind if they did.

Geography's impact on reporting can be seen in a study conducted by the Youth Media Council of Oakland, California. The council examined local newspaper coverage of housing issues for three months in 2007. Its report, *Displacing the dream*, shows how differently reporters from mostly middle-class neighborhoods saw housing issues compared to the residents of poor neighborhoods undergoing redevelopment:

> Displacement [of the poor] and gentrification are not portrayed as problems in coverage of housing and development. Instead, housing market issues, including subprime lending and stagnation of the market, were the primary problems raised in coverage. Corporate-driven solutions, including market-rate housing and luxury retail development, overshadowed government- and community-driven solutions, including affordable housing creation and improved social services. The voices of government officials, corporate spokespeople, and other traditional experts dominated over the voices of community advocates and organizers at a rate of six-to-one. Residents appeared in coverage primarily as "scene-setters" who describe neighborhood conditions. Residents rarely appeared as experts who voice analysis or solutions. ...

> ... Discussion of race and racism was nearly absent from coverage, despite ... statistics showing that San Francisco and Oakland have lost nearly a

quarter of their African-American populations in the past five years. [17]

The YMC study illustrates how fault lines can overlap. Divisions based on race, class, and geography frequently reinforce each other.

Geographic biases *within* a nation, however, pale when compared to biases arising *between* nations. That's because every nation has a unique culture: a set of shared symbols, history, myths, language (or at least accent and idioms, mate!), and assumptions about how the world does, and should, operate. Americans, Germans, Chinese, Nigerians, Egyptians, and Brazilians all see the world somewhat differently from each other. (And, of course, all see it differently than the French!)

The nationality fault line is the most important one to take into account when the press interprets world affairs for American audiences. And news from abroad grows ever more consequential as the nation becomes more *inter*dependent on others with the exponential growth of world trade, finance, communication, and travel.[18]

Nowhere is the fault line of nationality wider and deeper than in coverage of war. Despite the First Amendment's specific protection of press freedom, throughout our history government officials have censored dispatches from the front and substituted propaganda. Editors and correspondents have often been happy to go along, mistaking — or more likely, masking — jingoism with patriotism.[19] Even the most professional journalist embedded with soldiers is likely to be swayed, if not by simple camaraderie, by dependence on them for his/er safety. And how about us? Don't we in the audience *want* to hear of valor and victory even though we *need* to know exactly what's going on, including pain and shame.

Coverage of important U.S. allies is also likely to reflect partisan bias when they are in conflict with non-allied nations. The Israeli-Palestinian struggle stands out, perhaps because nationalistic biases are reinforced by ethnic and religious affiliations. Grade the News (a project I directed that reported on news quality in the San Francisco Bay Area) analyzed front-page coverage of the conflict in the *San Jose Mercury News* for six months from April 1 to Sept. 30, 2002. We found that an Israeli death was 11 times more likely to make a front-page headline in San Jose than a Palestinian fatality.[20]

The priority given to Israeli suffering in front-page headlines was reinforced throughout the stories by the order in which casualties were described, and first-person accounts of Israeli deaths contrasted with second-hand and approximate estimates of Palestinian fatalities. We also noticed that Palestinian forces were consistently labeled as "gunmen" and "militants" — terms with negative connotations in our culture — but rarely as "fighters" and never as "resistance forces," despite references to Palestinian cities as "the occupied territories." (I consider the designation of "terrorist" for suicide and car- bombers who kill civilians appropriate, but it also applies to states when they target non-combatants or kill indiscriminately.)

During the same period, we also monitored headlines of Middle East stories moved by the Associated Press, which most American newspapers relied on to cover the conflict. In its headlines, Israeli deaths were twice as likely to be mentioned as Palestinian ones.

Marda Dunsky, a professor at Northwestern University's Medill School of Journalism, illuminated the disparity in a book called *Pens and swords: How the American mainstream media report the Israeli-Palestinian conflict*. In her view, neutral standards of news judgment are sometimes trumped by three factors. First, Americans tend to identify with Israel and Israelis more than with Arab nations and Palestinians. Israel is a frequent travel destination for Americans, especially Jews and Christians who consider it the Holy Land. Second, she said, Israel comes closer to democratic ideals than Arab nations. Third, because American foreign policy treats Israel as a special ally, Americans tend to as well.

Cultural ties between Americans and Israelis can also affect the language choices reporters make, according to Dr. Dunsky. The name of the Palestinian group HAMAS is an acronym, she explained. The M stands for a word that translates to mean "resistance." Yet Palestinian fighters are almost never referred to as "the resistance."

Elise Ackerman, who covered the Israeli-Palestinian conflict for the *Mercury News* before the study period, elaborated on what she now considers her cross-cultural blindness:

> I couldn't believe that I hadn't used the term 'resistance' in my stories. There's been a resistance throughout the Arab world. It's a resistance to colonizers. I think that whole idea is missing from the coverage of the Palestinian conflict, because there is a resistance of Americans and Israelis to see the Israelis as colonizers, and that creates a problem with the use of the term.
>
> I do know in hindsight that the Palestinians do see this as resistance. The translator may not have provided the nuances. In hindsight I think I did really get lost.[21]

The fault line of geography helps us inquire whether a story might have been told quite differently by someone from a different place, especially a different nation. We can ask, *Is our viewpoint, or the information-provider's, biased by geography? Are there sources quoted presenting different perspectives based on where people live? Which viewpoints are marginalized or missing?*

The fault line of gender

If you've ever banged your head against the wall after talking to a colleague or family-member of the opposite sex, you've already stumbled over this fault line. The linguist

Deborah Tannen says the differences in the way men and women use language are so great it's cross-cultural, as if an American were speaking with a Japanese.[22]

"Nowhere," Professor Tannen wrote, "is the conflict between femininity and authority more crucial than with women in politics. If a man appears forceful, logical, direct, masterful, and powerful, he enhances his value as a man." If a woman embodies these characteristics, "she risks undercutting her value as a woman."[23]

In February 2008, *New York Times* columnist Nicholas Kristof described how gender differences were affecting Hillary Clinton's campaign for president:

> In one common experiment, the 'Goldberg paradigm,' people are asked to evaluate a particular article or speech, supposedly by a man. Others are asked to evaluate the identical presentation, but from a woman. Typically, in countries all over the world, the very same words are rated higher coming from a man.
>
> In particular, one lesson from this research is that promoting their own successes is a helpful strategy for ambitious men. But experiments have demonstrated that when women highlight their accomplishments, that's a turn-off. And women seem even more offended by self-promoting females than men are.
>
> This creates a huge challenge for ambitious women in politics or business: If they're self-effacing, people find them unimpressive, but if they talk up their accomplishments, they come across as pushy braggarts.[24]

Gender exerts bias not just in differences in content, but in which topics are considered newsworthy. Domestic and intimate partner violence, for example, has been a more frequent news story as women have increased their numbers and clout in newsrooms. Kim Barker, a reporter for the investigative journalism Web site *Pro Publica*, notes that women reporters "do a pretty good job of covering what it's like to live in a war zone, not just die in one." She wrote:

> Without female correspondents in war zones, the experiences of women there may be only a rumor. Look at the articles about women who set themselves on fire in Afghanistan to protest their arranged marriages, or about girls being maimed by fundamentalists, about child marriage in India, about rape in Congo and Haiti. Female journalists often tell those stories in the most compelling ways, because abused women are sometimes more comfortable talking to them. And those stories are at least as important as accounts of battles."[25]

So the fault line of gender prompts us to ask, *Is our viewpoint, or the information provider's, biased by gender? Does their information discount, stereotype, patronize, or belittle women, or men? Do the sources they reference differ by gender? Which viewpoints are marginalized or missing?*

The fault line of generation

Every generation seems to consider the one before, and eventually the one after, as less informed or at least less sophisticated than itself. (You feel me?)

The news media seem very aware of generational stereotypes: the selfless "greatest generation," the self-absorbed "baby boomers," "Gen X," "Gen Y," "Millennials," even "Gen Next." Generalizations about such age groupings are often applied to everyone within them, despite great individual differences. The most common generational bias, however, is ageism, the tendency to discount the importance of young people's or old people's points of view.

The fault line of generation encourages us to ask, *Is our viewpoint, or the information provider's, biased by age? Does their report discount or stereotype the young or old? Do the sources differ by generation? Whose viewpoints are privileged and whose discounted or ignored?*

The fault lines of other group cultures

I would add a sixth catchall category of perception benders – group cultures. Religions, ethnic identities, even professions, exercise a gravitational pull toward group-think – a condition in which those within a group echo and thereby reinforce an interpretation of reality common to the group.

> "We tend to be extremely tribal. We tend to like to cohere into groups. And we like perfect group loyalty."[26]
>
> ~ *New York Times* columnist David Brooks

In a *New York Times* article, the University of Virginia's Professor Haidt described bias in his own community of supposedly objective social psychologists: "If a group circles around sacred values, they will evolve into a tribal-moral community. They'll embrace science whenever it supports their sacred values, but they'll ditch it or distort it as soon as it threatens a sacred value." Dr. Haidt noted that it's easy for social scientists to observe this process in *other* communities, such as fundamentalist Christians who reject evolution in favor of "intelligent design." But academics do the same thing, as Harvard sociologist Daniel Patrick Moynihan found in 1965 when he warned about the rise of unmarried parenthood and welfare dependency among blacks — violating the taboo against criticizing victims of racism.[27]

This fault line encourages us to ask: *Is our viewpoint, or the information provider's, biased by cultural groupings? Does the news report discount or stereotype cultural out-groups as inferior or even as enemies? Do the sources differ by cultural group? Which groups' viewpoints are privileged and which are discounted or missing, even when the story concerns them?*

Robert Maynard's insights about social fault lines make a compelling case for diversity both of sources quoted in news and among journalists themselves.

Most of the layers of bias outlined in this chapter have been *personal* – belonging to us and those who inform us. In the next chapter we'll examine an even more powerful type of bias – the self-interest of the *institution* providing news or information.

4

The Covert Bias of Institutions

The press ... is caught between its desire to please and extend its audience and its desire to give a picture of events and people as they really are.

~ The Commission on Freedom of the Press[1]

When I was a young journalist I worked for a newspaper in the red-clay foothills of western South Carolina. It was cotton mill country in the mid-1970s. At one end of the mill, walnut-sized cotton balls were separated from their dried husks and combed into thread that was then woven by hundreds of clanking looms into the towels and sheets that probably graced your parents' home. The air was hot and thick with dust and lint. It settled on the looms like a downy coat, making them look like frantic birds. It nestled in the hair of the workers, who were sometimes derided as "lint heads."

The finer particles of cotton dust accumulated in workers' lungs causing a disease called "brown lung" — more formally, byssinosis — that shortened the breath and lives of many millworkers. Consulting the Occupational Safety and Health Administration, OSHA, I discovered that not a single mill in the county my newspaper served was even close to healthy air quality standards. Seemed like a pretty important story. Indeed, it won the coveted Pulitzer Prize for Public Service in 1981.

But I didn't get to write it. My first investigative article was my last. The editor who put it on the front page was fired the following week. The publisher never said why he killed the series. But textile manufacturing was the dominant local industry, employing almost 400,000 people in the piedmont of the two Carolinas. If a newspaper made a stink about unhealthy mills, OSHA might grow teeth. The once-stream-powered red-brick mills of the South were old. The cost of cleaning them up might have exceeded the cost of abandoning them for modern mills constructed beyond the U.S. border, where labor was even cheaper and health regulations even less binding. Were western Carolina's mills shuttered, the loss of so many jobs would have thrown the local economy into recession. My newspaper's advertising revenue would have plummeted. Exposing the health risk to so many workers might have been a life and breath story, but it put the paper's considerable profits at risk. Fortunately, a more socially responsible newspaper, the *Charlotte* (N.C.) *Observer*, conducted an extensive investigation and won the Pulitzer Prize and a trophy case of other awards.[2]

The lesson? Information-providers often face a conflict between their self-interest and the public interest.

The institutions — governments, non-profits, corporations, and especially news media — that produce most of what we know about current events[3] can mute but not moot most of the *individual* prejudices described in chapter 3 by employing a sufficiently diverse and collaborative staff. But institutions exert their own overarching self-interest, which can be imposed on the behavior of their employees. Particularly for profit-seeking institutions, their short-term self-interest *conflicts more than coincides* with the purpose of socially responsible journalism. Most corporations seek to maximize profit rather than maximizing public understanding of those current issues and events with the greatest impact on the community served.

Companies offering shares on the stock market are legally *required* to optimize value for their investors. Privately held media firms — and those with protected classes of voting stock — enjoy greater flexibility, but *all* institutions look out for themselves. Government agencies, even non-profit organizations, are focused, if not on growth, on their own survival. An institution eager to put itself out of business is as rare as an exterminator who would welcome the extinction of termites.

Institutional information-providers — just like individuals — are loath to admit any conflict between their own self-interest and the audience's interest in obtaining truth, the whole truth and nothing but the truth. Candor would undermine their effectiveness. Advertising is most persuasive when it appears to be purely informational. To be believed, press agents present themselves as honest information brokers. And news media that lose their credibility risk losing their audience. So they are forever boasting that they report "objectively," "without fear or favor" or that they are "fair and balanced."[4]

"The language of advertising and public relations is meant to seduce you into buying or believing something."[5]

Steve Inskeep, host of NPR's Morning Edition

No one should be surprised that job #1 for advertisers is to boost sales rather than public knowledge of goods and services (or candidates for office). Nor should it come as a shock that public relations practitioners are advocates paid to make their clients look as good as plausible, not to be impartial fact-finders. When processing ads or PR, our skepticism shields should be set close to 100%. News media, on the other hand, almost universally claim selfless dedication to informing the public.[6] Therefore this chapter will center on four propositions concerning bias in news organizations:

1. From the *New York Times* to Fox News to NPR, every organization providing news or information suffers from a conflict of interest.

2. These conflicts of interest are growing more intrusive as traditional news media hemorrhage resources and new providers emerge.

3. Commercial bias occurs when information providers put their own welfare ahead of their audience's. It expresses itself primarily in four ways: (1) pandering to the audience's prejudices or whimsy; (2) displacing substance with sensation; (3) shaping content to suit advertisers; and (4) letting corporate and government publicists set the news agenda or supply its content.

4. Commercial bias represents a greater threat to democracy than liberal or conservative bias.

All communication is based on an exchange

We rarely think of personal communication in economic terms. But when we provide others with news or information face-to-face or at a digital water cooler such as Facebook, whether we're aware of it or not, we are participating in an *exchange*. We provide information we think will interest them. In return, we receive their attention (which humans always crave) and the chance to influence them with what we say, write or share. No money changes hands, but they "pay" attention. So we're getting something increasingly scarce and valuable. Like all voluntary exchanges, neither party would engage if they didn't believe something were in it for them.

In addition to this beneficial side of such exchanges, there can be a downside because most of the time each party is seeking its own ends, not altruistically satisfying the other's needs. While our audience may wish to know the truth in order to make the best decisions, more often than we care to admit, we exaggerate or embellish or selectively inform or flatter. Or worse. In a word, we often try to manipulate our audience, even if only to get and keep their attention.

To see how your self-interest can interfere with factual communication, try this thought experiment: Let's say you're married or living with a romantic partner. Now imagine you're at a party without your main squeeze and an attractive stranger strikes up a conversation. Sensing interest in a relationship, do you alert them to your existing partnership — something they would clearly want to know — or do you kindle the sparks of a flirtation? You may have no intention of starting a fire, but who doesn't want to feel attractive?

Or a police officer pulls you over and asks how fast you were going? Or how much you've been drinking? Or your sweetie pie asks, "Have I gained some weight?" Honesty may be the best policy, but it can cost you. If we're honest with ourselves — perhaps the most painful place in which to recognize truth — we often let our self-interest influence our communications with others.

So do institutions.

1. Every organization providing news or information suffers from a conflict of interest

Unlike the exchange between two persons, other unseen parties exert a powerful influence on communication between an institution and members of an audience.

To begin with, a news organization must answer not to a single person, but compete for a mass audience in a marketplace. Next, commercial media, the dominant type in American journalism, must follow priorities set and enforced not by journalists or professional communicators, but by profit-seeking owners or a board of directors running a corporation competing in a market for investors. And because most media rely on advertisers for a substantial part of their revenue, retailers also shape content, though usually subtly. Finally, sources of information — those who supply the raw material for the production of news — exert influence. Together these comprise market pressures.

What about individual journalists? After all, they conduct the reporting, take the pictures, and produce the content. What becomes news must pass through their eyes, ears and — one hopes — brains. That does give them a say, but despite their longing for independent professional status, journalists are much more decision-takers than decision-makers.[7] They are cooks, not chefs — employees who do what they're told or risk their jobs. In *Media Ethics*, Professor Conrad Fink gives journalists this blunt advice: "Either you and the hand that feeds you agree on ethics in reporting and writing, or you (not your editor) will be a very unhappy employee — or unemployed."[8]

Thus the news, which seems like the creation of a single journalist, is really an elaborate compromise.[9] It's a bit like a puppet being pulled simultaneously by four puppeteers. Owners hold the thickest string, followed by advertisers, sources, and the mass audience. The slack in the strings constitutes the journalist's autonomy.

From each of these markets a conflict arises between the public interest and the self-interest of the news provider:[10]

> • Rational **owners** seeking to maximize profit should produce whatever content generates the largest audience attractive to advertisers at the lowest cost. But often the information most essential to the public interest is expensive to gather (e.g. investigative reporting). It may offend major employers (such as the textile industry), advertisers, or sources (if their faults are publicized) or alienate some segments of the audience (if it punctures popular myths or exposes a popular leader's flaws). Content that maximizes public understanding tends to *minimize* profits, at least in the short run.[11]

• Rational **advertisers** seek the largest audience of *potential customers* at the least cost, in the most favorable context — one that uncritically excites interest in acquiring those goods and services on offer. Audiences with money to spend, particularly those in the peak buying ages from 18 to 54, are the most likely to become customers. Advertisers will pay a premium for their eyeballs. But the common good is not advanced by selecting news designed to appeal primarily to the demographic segments of the community that advertisers value most. News ought to be more than bait.

Democracies require information that's responsive to the information needs of *all* citizens in the community, regardless of customer potential. Nor is the public interest served by content designed to stoke interest in advertised goods and services. Rather, the public requires trustworthy information about those issues and events most powerfully shaping its environment. Such news rarely addresses the thrill of owning a backyard spa, wall-sized TV or sporty SUV. Content tailored to answer the entire community's questions about current events, rather than to attract the most advertising dollars, generates lower rates of profit.

• Rational **sources** — from athletes to business execs to politicians — reward news media that they believe portray them fairly — i.e. uncritically — with scoops and access.[12] Sources who relish critical coverage are as common as vegetarian sharks. Sources punish those whom they perceive as unfair by denying or delaying access. They may not return phone calls. When news providers serve the public interest by holding the powerful to account, they may be making it more effortful — and therefore expensive — to gather news.

- The **audience:** You and I, dear reader, may *not* be paragons of rational self-interest. We may favor softer, simpler stories over more substantive content. Who is not tempted by titillation? Immune from the allure of lurid tales of violent crime? Unfazed by celebrity? Unmoved by stories aimed like Cupid's bow at our heartstrings, but bypassing our brains? Likewise, who applauds coverage of *our* side's faults? Who favors complexity and nuance over simplicity and brevity? Who has the time and idealism to keep up with news of civic import when we each have only a single vote, one say in thousands at the most local level and in a hundred million at the national? Who needs the trouble? You and I may make it more profitable to provide the news we *want* than the news we *need*.

Even non-commercial news providers, such as National Public Radio, face three of these market influences. Liberation from the unrelenting pressure to earn the rising levels of profit investors covet is no small thing. But non-profits must more than break even to expand or ensure their future. For that they rely significantly on advertisers (whom they call underwriters). Those advertisers pay based on how many potential customers are attracted to the content, just as they do for profit-seeking news media. Non-profits must also attract a mass of users willing to donate, just as for-profit media seek subscribers. And non-profits face pressure to report delicately about the interests of those who can write big checks, just as for-profits worry about offending major advertisers. Like all journalists, those working for non-profits also rely on access to news-making sources. Regardless of employer, a journalist can only be as good as his/er sources.

"We need to run our businesses like businesses, even if our goal is public service rather than profitability."[13]

~ John Thornton, chairman of the *Texas Tribune*, an online non-profit news organization specializing in covering state politics

Some news organizations surrender to these market forces squeezing the newsroom. Most compromise. Some resist. But none can ignore their demands. Nor can we, if we hope to avoid being fooled.

2. These conflicts of interest are growing more intrusive as traditional news media hemorrhage resources and new providers emerge

The demise of mainstream news

As recently as 2000, news media were among the most profitable businesses in the nation. Newspaper profits routinely exceeded 20 percent return on very substantial gross revenues. That's about three times the profitability of average American companies. Even with such high profit demands, there was money to spend on substantial reporting staffs, investigations, and prize-winning journalism. But by 2010, newspapers' profitability had shriveled and several large chains were bankrupt. Some had silenced their presses. Tens of thousands of journalists had lost their jobs.[14] *New York Times* publisher Arthur Sulzberger Jr. described the situation for American newspapers as "the most disruptive transition in the history of mass communications."[15]

Similar gales have buffeted television. The general manager at a San Francisco network affiliated station told me in the mid-1980s that a monkey sitting in his seat could guarantee a 50% annual profit on revenues. "My job," he said, "is to beat the monkey."[16] But those salad days have wilted. Stations have severely cut staff to preserve much smaller profits. Network broadcasters have suffered even greater attrition.

Before the World Wide Web was invented, store owners had to pay whatever newspapers asked to reach local customers with the kind of price and product detail that print does better than broadcast. For the motivational ads TV does so well, they had to bargain with a handful of broadcast stations, bidding against each other for limited ad time on popular programs like newscasts.

But then companies such as Google offered advertisers direct access to potential customers for pennies on the dollar traditional media charged. What better place to sell a lawnmower than next to a consumer's search for that word? Craigslist offered for free classified ads that used to cost hundreds of dollars. Firms like Monster.com made it easier to list and search for jobs, depleting scores of pages of employment ads each week. On top of that, most newspapers offered everything they put in print, on screen, for free.[17] Readers didn't even have to lug the paper out to the recycling bin. Is it any surprise that paid circulation plummeted?

Advertisers had paid for everything in broadcast and contributed upwards of 80% of newspapers' revenue.[18] But their willingness to subsidize journalism vanished faster than virtue in Vegas. Media firms have cut their ad rate cards as deeply as staff. Journalists didn't know what hit them. In 2009 when the presses of Denver's 150-year-old *Rocky Mountain News* rumbled for the final time, a newly unemployed reporter wrote: "I feel like a blacksmith in 1915. I didn't lose my job; I lost my career."[19]

Resource-poor journalism

As newsrooms empty, news content is changing. Some wonderful journalism continues to be broadcast, published, and posted.[20] But over the past decade, sensation has been gradually displacing substance. Instead of using their talents to make the important interesting, news media often are making what's merely interesting *seem* important by playing it on page one and at the top of newscasts and Web sites.

"I think the press has become much more trivial."[21]

~ *New Yorker* media writer Ken Auletta

There appears to be less coverage of important issues, especially of what state and local governments are doing with our tax dollars. In 2009 *American Journalism* Review surveyed the number of newspaper reporters who cover state capitols and "found a staggering loss of reporting firepower" since the last survey in 2003. There were 32 percent fewer full time reporters covering statehouses.[22] In California, a series of interviews in 2007 with 62 leaders from across the state – including top journalists, educators, and heads of civic organizations and state government – was conducted by the California Media Project. It concluded:

> Nearly four out of five people we interviewed felt that the media in California are doing only a 'fair' or 'poor' job covering critical issues facing the state. Almost as many felt the quality of coverage has deteriorated in recent years. There was a strong sense that personalities drive media coverage — what several referred to as the "Paris Hilton" effect.[23]

"I'm discouraged by the fact that radio and television — and to some extent even newspapers — faced with a shrinking market, tend to go more and more for sensation, for scandal, for murders and sex stories and so on ... ."[24]

~ The late Daniel Schorr, long-time CBS foreign correspondent and NPR senior analyst.

California is not atypical. In its overview of American journalism, *The state of the media 2008* reported:

> A comprehensive audit of coverage shows that in 2007 ... what wasn't covered was in many ways as notable as what was. Other than Iraq — and to a lesser degree Pakistan and Iran — there was minimal coverage of events

overseas, some of which directly involved U.S. interests, blood, and treasure. At the same time, consider the list of the domestic issues that each filled less than a single percent of the news hole: education, race, religion, transportation, the legal system, housing, drug trafficking, gun control, welfare, Social Security, aging, labor, abortion, and more.

And newer media seem to have an even narrower peripheral vision than older media. Cable news, talk radio (and also blogs) tend to seize on top stories (often polarizing ones) and amplify them. The Internet offers the promise of aggregating ever more sources, but its value still depends on what those originating sources are providing. Even as the media world has fragmented into more outlets and options, reporting resources have shrunk.[25]

A 2008 national survey of journalists conducted by the Pew Research Center concluded:

An ever larger majority of journalists at national media outlets (62%) says that journalism is going in the wrong direction, an increase from the 51% who expressed this view in 2004. Half of Internet journalists and about the same proportion of local journalists (49%) also take a negative view of the state of their profession.[26]

Media consolidation

In 2000, reporters for different news outlets competed with each other to report new information in many metro areas. Competing newsrooms are generally more aggressive news-gatherers than monopoly operations. More importantly, the sacred cows and blind spots of one newsroom might be exposed by another.[27] But the drain of advertising dollars has acted like a black hole, sucking once-independent newspapers into thinly-staffed clusters of nearby papers under single ownership that barely emit light.[28] Television stations now cooperate on local news almost as often as they compete.[29] While consumers are now able to seek *global* and *national* news from more sources than ever, mainstream *local* news in most markets has become more of a monotone.

"All of this consolidation that we had been through had led to closing of newsrooms, firing of reporters. Right now we've got thousands and thousands of reporters who are walking the streets in search of a job and they should be walking the beats in search of a story."[30]

~ Michael J. Copps, former Federal Communications Commission member

New sources of news

Some new journalism outlets emerging on the Internet are promising. Following a nonprofit model, Voice of San Diego (www.voiceofsandiego.org) has broken important local stories with a staff of only 11. Talking Points Memo, (www. talkingpointsmemo. com) with fewer than 20 staff members and interns, has become a go-to site for politics. Foundation-backed Pro Publica (www.propublica.org) in New York City aims to produce investigative reports that would be offered free to traditional news media.[31] Politico.com offers insightful original reporting on national politics.

Still, only a handful of these newcomers rival even small daily newspapers in depth, professionalism, or number of journalists. Far more common is news and commentary on the Internet produced by *non*-journalists. "Businesses themselves are rapidly becoming 'publishers,' filling the void with 'news' they generate about themselves and then merrily distribute on the web," according to Ken Doctor, lead news analyst for Outsell and former Knight Ridder Digital news executive.[32]

> "I don't think that democratization of news-gathering is necessarily, in and of itself, a good thing."[33]
>
> ~ Ted Koppel, former anchor of ABC's Nightline and current NPR senior news analyst

Jan Schaffer, a former newspaper journalist who now heads J-Lab, a project supported by the John S. and James L. Knight Foundation to foster innovations in Web-based journalism, directed a study of citizen media. She described several commonalities among a very diverse crop of citizen media:

- They depend for their vitality on citizens sharing their thoughts, observations, and experiences. Subjectivity prevails.

- Citizens for the most part do not desire to contribute fully reported articles with leads, middles, and ends, or to communicate their experiences in polished essay form (though some do). Many sites boast volunteer columnists. In a few cities, such as Madison, Wisconsin, professionals are trying to train citizens to become journalists. But there is little evidence that many civilians want to call around and conduct interviews.[34]

The conflicts of interest impinging on established media don't vanish for the citizen journalist or blogger. These individuals also want to expand their audience, attract and retain advertisers and have officials return phone calls. But they typically lack the training and resources of journalists and may not be aware of the craft's ethical standards. They can't afford editors to check facts or restrain biases. A one-person staff *can't* be diverse. And the person selling the ads is often also reporting the news — cross-purposes that only someone with a split personality could manage. Conflicts of interest are, in fact, more common when citizen journalists have day jobs and connections with the subjects they report on. And those divided loyalties may not be disclosed. We may not know that the blogger covering the neighborhood school presents the principal in a dim light not for poor leadership but because she disciplined the blogger's son.

3. Commercial bias occurs when information providers put their own welfare ahead of their audience's. It expresses itself primarily in four ways:

(1) pandering to the audience's prejudices or whimsy;

(2) displacing substance with sensation;

(3) shaping content to suit advertisers; and

(4) letting corporate and government publicists set the news agenda or supply its content

"It is these forces of commercialism which now provide the greatest obstacle to truth-telling journalism."[35]

British journalist Nick Davies, author of *Flat Earth News*

Think of news media as society's headlights. They can't smooth a bumpy road, but they can help us steer around obstacles and avoid plunging off a cliff. That is, if they are bright and aimed at the path ahead. Commercial bias dims the lights so we can't make out ruinous practices on Wall Street before the world's economy crashes. Commercial bias directs the spotlight of public attention away from the road, perhaps to illuminate a couple necking in the woods or young men playing with a ball.

Pandering

The quote at the top of this chapter from the Commission on Freedom of the Press refers to first type of commercial bias in news — slanting the news to maximize audience rather than public understanding. Writing in 1947, the Commission noted that "People seldom want to read or hear about what does not please them; they seldom want others to read or hear about what disagrees with their convictions or what presents an unfavorable picture of groups they belong to"(p. 57). This creates great pressure to pander to public prejudices rather than challenge them.

A half century ago this type of commercial bias was evident when most newspapers and television stations in the South during the struggle for civil rights portrayed African-Americans' campaign for equality as lawless or worse, when they reported on it at all.[36]

From 9/11/2001 to March, 2003 many news outlets, including some of the most prestigious, avoided critical coverage of the Bush administration's case for invading Iraq. The strategy avoided charges of being unpatriotic and thus risking loss of audience. In his 2008 memoir, Scott McClellan, the White House press secretary at the time, called the media "complicit enablers" in the administration's effort to sell the war.[37] Katie Couric, the first woman to anchor the CBS Evening News, agreed. On CBS' Early Show, Ms. Couric called the period, "one of the most embarrassing chapters in American journalism." At the time, when she was working as host of NBC's "Today Show," she said she felt pressure from "the corporations who own where we work and from the government itself to really squash any kind of dissent or any kind of questioning of it."[38] The Fox News Channel went so far as to brand all of its coverage of the invasion with the logo "Operation Iraqi Freedom," using the Bush administration's partisan label rather than maintaining the independent stance required in codes of journalism ethics.

Today the willingness to mold coverage in order to please and expand audience is exemplified by talk radio hosts such as Michael Savage (born Michael Alan Weiner) and Rush Limbaugh. Fox News Channel commentators such as Bill O'Reilly, Sean Hannity and Sarah Palin are less extreme, but adopt a conservative viewpoint that contrasts with Fox's "fair and balanced" logo. (Until he resigned in 2009, Keith Olbermann played to a liberal audience on MSNBC, but there was no pretense of neutrality or balance. On the same network, Rachel Maddow has adopted an openly liberal, but civil, approach to news commentary.)

From a mass to a niche market

Before the mid-1990s, when there were only four national networks, leaning to one side or another of the political spectrum would have made little economic sense. A conservative or liberal slant would have alienated too many viewers. But now, thanks to cable and satellite TV as well as streaming video on the Web, the market for national news and comment is crowded. Such markets favor niche programming. A network like Fox can gather more audience by owning the allegiance of conservatives than by competing with CNN, ABC, NBC, CBS, PBS, NPR and the Web sites of the *New York Times*, the *Washington Post* and others for an increasingly small slice of the middle of the political spectrum. Online, the *Huffington Post* appears to be using the same niche strategy on the left.[39]

'Click candy'

A second type of pandering is apolitical. It gives prominence to whatever catches the public imagination, no matter how trivial. Online editors call it "click candy." Web masters can count their own site visitors in real time and scan Google Trends (http://www.google.com/trends) and the "most popular" or "most shared" sections of major news Web sites to tailor the news to what's hot at the moment.

"Favoring subjects already trending high in online interest is called search engine optimization," explained Bob Garfield, co-host of NPR's On the Media program. "Another term might be 'auto-pandering.'"[40] No matter what it's called, advertisers pay more to be seen on sites with lots of visitors. Such sites also come up higher in Google searches, generating even greater popularity to sell ads against.

Although the Web makes it easier, playing to the audience's whimsy is nothing new. At a news literacy conference in 2009, the former president of CBS News Andrew Heyward said, "Let's not kid ourselves... there are a lot of examples of journalism that are driven by pure circulation considerations that clearly could be called pandering."[41]

"If you use popularity in any form, surveys or hit counts, for what stories you run, that leads to a universe where we're in two wars and two economic crises and what you see or read is basically about celebrities and political yelling."[42]

~ Radio satirist and The Simpsons' voice actor Harry Shearer

Sensationalism

Sensationalism is a conscious effort to boost audience by choosing — and often exaggerating — events likely to stir emotion — especially fear, surprise, sorrow, anger, or titillation — at the expense of more newsworthy occurrences. Sensationalism can also contaminate *presentation* — focusing on the provocative aspects of important events and issues while ignoring or downplaying the substantive.

Sensationalism has long plagued news media. In 1870 Mark Twain observed that "the first great end and aim of journalism is to make a *sensation*. Never let your paper go to press without a sensation. If you have none, make one." (Emphasis in original).[43] Newspapers became more professional during most of the 20th century, adopting standards of ethics, hiring better educated journalists, and diminishing sensationalism. But since the mid-1980s, greater demand for profit from Wall Street investors and the advent of cable news and the Web have brought sensationalism roaring back.[44]

Selecting stories for sensation

The most obvious examples of choosing sensation over substance are stories about celebrities and saturation coverage of shocking episodes of violent crime. O.J. Simpson combined the two and dominated coverage for more than a year. Missing blondes and murdered children — especially when the mom is suspected — are popular. So are the peccadilloes of celebrities such as Charlie Sheen, Lindsay Lohan and those cleavish Kardashians. Some local TV stations have hired angry shouters such as Bubba the Love Sponge (WTSP, St. Petersburg) and JoAnn Augello, "the real housewife of Bensonhurst" (WNYW, New York) to rant for ratings.[45]

Prepping for a public lecture on April 4, 2010, I opened Google's news page to check on the news media's priorities. At the time Congress was vigorously debating reform of the nation's health care system. And a golfer named Tiger Woods had been accused of infidelity. The following chart shows the number of articles mentioning Mr. Woods, Congresswoman Nancy Pelosi, leader of the Democrats in the House, Senate Democrat leader Harry Reid, Senate Republican leader Mitch McConnell and House Republican leader John Boehner, the principal antagonists in the debate. [46]

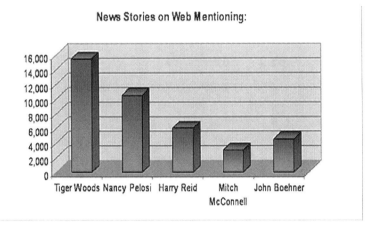

News Stories on Web Mentioning:

(Lest you be tempted to add the politicians' blocks to estimate overall coverage of the health care debate, you should know that the same story often appeared in more than one politician's tallies, as reporters collected comments from both sides of the aisle.)

Unless the Tiger has broadcast his seed more widely than reported, it's safe to say that his straying into the marital rough affected hundreds of millions fewer people than a sweeping overhaul of American health care. Quite aside from the *quantity* of coverage, *American Journalism Review* criticized its *quality*: "The mainstream media too often dropped sourcing standards and blindly followed the lead of the tabs and entertainment Web sites during the Tiger Woods extravaganza."[47]

Coverage of celebrities has almost zero value in orienting us to reality or helping us make wise collective or personal decisions. Yes, it may empower chit-chat at the water cooler. Or confirm some danger your parents warned about. But otherwise, such stories are simply nonfiction entertainment. Lurid crime and gossip sell, however, and are usually cheap to report. Police and publicists do most of the work and provide the information free. Publicity-seeking, self-proclaimed experts are happy to fill time on cable television news without charge, speculating about cases that have sparked public curiosity. From a short-term economic standpoint, sensation has a great benefit-to-cost ratio.

Los Angeles Times sports columnist Bill Dwyre put the opportunistic nature of celebrity-chasing in perspective:

> Our society has a massive appetite for drama, and little for reality. We read about Britney Spears when we need to read about Afghanistan. And the media, which [have] the mandate — and the constitutional right — to lead us from this abyss, are all too often not doing so. Media, which once led public opinion, now all too often follow it.

> We aren't just talking celebrity scandal sheets, weekly shoppers and sports-talk radio. Last week, a Los Angeles bureau executive of the Associated Press, no less, put out a memo to staff that said they were to pay more attention to developments about Britney Spears. The message was: She is news.

> No she isn't. She is titillation. She is a troubled young woman whom we cover with delight, rather than empathy. She is web hits, the current fool's gold of the newspaper industry.[48]

Coverage of celebrities and episodes of violence, however, represents just the tip of the sensationalism iceberg. Any person or thing that's quirky or elicits strong emotional reaction can become "newsworthy" if it promises to attract mass attention at little cost. Often it's someone from the local community who does something extraordinary or outrageous.

"News outlets have a very strong interest to find the sexy tidbit that makes it interesting to turn to the news."[49]

~ Lawrence Lessig, Harvard Law School professor

An example from the San Francisco Bay Area concerns one Anna Ayala, a little-known grifter. Little-known, that is, until she found an ingenious use for the tip of a finger her husband had brought home from work. The decaying digit had come into his possession after an industrial accident involving a co-worker. Ms. Ayala submerged the finger in a steaming bowl of Wendy's chili and then feigned visceral disgust. (She hadn't ordered finger food!) Protesting that the fast-food chain had taken a short cut in its preparation of *con carne*, she threatened to file a lawsuit. Lots of money would settle her stomach and quell her anguish.

Thirty-three days passed from the first media report of the finger in the chili to the weekend of her arrest for fraud. At the time, March to April 2005, a violent revolt against American forces was springing up in Iraq. The U.S. was frantically trying to put together a government in that fractured land. On the home front, Democrats accused the Bush administration of attempting to "privatize" social security. Congressional Republicans were crafting an energy bill giving massive subsidies to oil companies that were already reaping record profits. The controversy over U.S. soldiers torturing and sexually humiliating Iraqi prisoners at Abu Ghraib was at full boil. North Korea was building long-range missiles and boasting of nuclear weapons. A would-be Al Qaeda airline hijacker, Zacarias Moussaoui, was being tried. In short, lots of newsworthy stuff was going on.

How often do you think the two-time Pulitzer Prize-winning *San Jose Mercury News* chose the finger-in-the-chili-bowl story for its front page during those 33 days?

Eleven. It was in the paper a total of 23 times, including an editorial.

How often did the war, or any story about Iraq, crack the front page during that 33-day period?

Once. And that was a story about a single person, a beautiful, idealistic, young woman from the San Francisco Bay

Area who ran a charity in Baghdad until she died in a roadside bombing.

How about the attempt to form a new Iraqi government? Abu Ghraib? Social Security "privatization?" The energy bill? North Korea? Moussaoui's trial? *Nada.* Not once in 33 days.[50]

Why tell people so much about something so insignificant on the most-read page of a newspaper that was once rated among the top ten in the nation? Because the story had "buzz." Editors could tell from counting Web site hits on its articles about the scam. It was also cheap. Not only were police providing information, but reporters from other news organizations – operating on commercial logic similar to the *Mercury's* – were finding out tidbits about Ms. Ayala's colorful past. Once reported, other media could use them for free.

There's no question the finger-in-the-chili case was bizarre and interesting. It deserved some coverage. But putting it on the front page so often pushed far more consequential stories to inside pages or entirely out of the paper.

> "If your goal is to return a profit to a shareholder, it's going to take you down a different path than if you are really looking at your work as enlightening, inspiring, educating the public."[51]
>
> ~ Paula Kerger, president of the Public Broadcasting System

Sensationalism in crafting the story

Even if a news organization selects important topics, a conflict between public service and media self-interest can still arise from *how the story is told*. Two related techniques predominate: exaggeration and overdramatization.

Exaggeration

To boost audience, news tellers are constantly tempted to make more of the available facts than they merit. Have you ever come away from the evening newscast preparing for a flood only to experience a seasonal sprinkle? TV weathercasters trained at the "Chicken Little" school of meteorology have become commonplace on local newscasts. (Of course, global warming threatens to make such forecasts more accurate!)

"The press is our immune system. If it overreacts to everything, we actually get sicker...."[52]

~ Jon Stewart of The Daily Show

The "sky is falling" approach extends well beyond weather reports. Other kinds of news are hyped, often to generate fear or another primal emotion. Here's an example:

"When you go to the public restroom, is someone watching you?" That's how Channel 13 in Albuquerque teased its 10 o'clock newscast one evening in 1998. "It's called cruising, and 13 News discovered it's going on right here in New Mexico," the anchor warned, before adding fear of pedophilia. "Your children use public restrooms all the time ... Sometimes they even go in alone."

But the story, "Behind the walls of the stalls," as described in a 2007 book about local television news, came up empty. Channel 13 reporters checked out only three public restrooms from a Web site list of 50 around the state where men were said to meet. They found nothing. A search of police records yielded only two incidents of indecent exposure in the entire state. There was no evidence of pedophilia.[53]

Such exaggeration was common in local television news, particularly during "sweeps" months when audiences are measured to set advertising rates, according to the Project for Excellence in Journalism. PEJ analyzed more than 33,000 local TV news stories broadcast from 154 stations across the U.S. from 1998 to 2002.

While "Behind the Walls" represents blatant manipulation that more respectable news providers wouldn't stoop to, subtle exaggeration happens across the board.

When I was a reporter, I used to try to write stories to the hilt, getting every bit of larger meaning out of whatever I was covering. That's what I told myself. But I was also trying to get on the front page as often as possible to advance my career. Reporters' reputations —and salaries — are based on how often their stories are judged worthy of page one. And, of course, the more startling the news, the more people feel they have to read or watch to be in the know. Overplaying the news is more profitable for both the journalist and the news firm than underplaying it.

Overdramatization

Journalists are taught that the best way to make the important engaging is to inject human interest value in the news. "People-izing the news," they call the technique in local television newsrooms. News told with empathy makes us care about the people in the spotlight. It humanizes them, helping us see ourselves in them, and thus it can build community as well as audience. That's all to the good. The danger arises when dramatic storytelling overwhelms informing or when conflict is emphasized over consensus. Such drama in news is like spice. A little goes a long way. Too much and the orientational value of the story is spoiled.

Examples of this kind of commercial bias include the tendency to cover the most vociferous parties to a controversy more than the most substantive or those with the greatest public support. Conflict is an essential element of every drama. *Washington Post* columnist E.J. Dionne wrote this about coverage of town hall meetings held by members of Congress on health care reform in 2009:

> There is an overwhelming case that the electronic media went out of their way to cover the noise and ignored the calmer (and from television's point of view "boring") encounters between elected representatives and their constituents.

> It's also clear that the anger that got so much attention largely reflects a fringe right-wing view opposed to all sorts of government programs most Americans support. Much as the far left of the antiwar movement commanded wide coverage during the

> Vietnam years, so now are extremists on the right hogging the media stage — with the media's complicity.[54]

Calvin tells Hobbes: "Conflict is *drama*. Drama is entertaining and entertainment is marketable. Finding consensus and common ground is *dull*. Nobody wants to watch a civilized discussion that acknowledges ambiguity and complexity. We want to see fireworks!

"We want the sense of solidarity and identity that comes from having our interests narrowed and exploited by like-minded zealots!

"Talk show hosts, political candidates, news programs, special interest groups... They all become successful by reducing debates to the level of shouted rage. Nothing gets solved, but we're all entertained."[55]

~ Cartoonist Bill Watterson

In all its varied forms, sensationalism contributes to a culture of entertainment that's incapable of confronting the complexity we face as technology accelerates change and as the people of the world become increasingly interdependent.

A caveat

Sensationalism only characterizes stories where consequence has been *displaced* by emotional appeal. Even titillating topics sometimes constitute legitimate news. When a president or another prominent politician cheats on a spouse, particularly if that politician emphasizes family values, the public is well-served by knowing it. A leader's private life becomes the public's business to the extent it reveals the person's fitness to conduct the public's business.

Shaping the news to attract or reward advertising

News execs often argue that they give the people what they want. The audience is in control, not them, and certainly not advertisers. But even though Glenn Beck more than doubled the audience for Fox News' 5 p.m. time slot and dominated his cable rivals, he was eased out after liberal groups organized an ad boycott of his program. "I think his ratings provided us, unfortunately, with empty calories, basically something that we could not monetize," conceded Roger Domal, vice president for eastern ad sales at Fox News in a *New York Times* interview.[56] Those who paid the piper called off Mr. Beck's tune.

In 2012 when Rush Limbaugh called a Georgetown University law student a "slut" and a "prostitute," for testifying before Congress that birth control pills ought to be covered by health insurance, he only offered an apology after advertisers began fleeing his program.

Advertiser boycotts are rare. But advertisers need not band together to shape news. Editors have a keen sense of what advertisers desire despite the fire wall journalism's ethical codes erect between advertising and news. The Society of

Professional Journalists' Code of Ethics states: "Distinguish news from advertising and shun hybrids that blur the lines between the two."[57] The idea is to protect consumers from being misled and the news provider from losing its credibility. But it's often profitable, at least in the short run, for news media to mix the two.

Pay-for-play

George Habit penned a column reviewing restaurants for the *San Francisco Examiner,* then owned by Philip Anschutz's Clarity Media Group. At Grade the News, the media watchdog Web site that I directed in the San Francisco Bay Area, we noticed that Mr. Habit's reviews were unfailingly positive and often referred to restaurants that advertised on the same or an adjoining page. When I called him about this he was surprisingly candid. He said he was primarily an ad salesman. "I use the column as an initiative to get advertisers to run an ad," he explained. Did his editors approve? "The paper gives me a free rein," he responded. So much so that only after we promised to expose the pay-for-play scheme did the *Examiner* agree to halt the scam.[58] We found similar stories-for-ads at the *Palo Alto Daily News,* part of a group of free Bay Area newspapers then owned by the prestigious Knight Ridder chain.[59]

The practice was not confined to small papers, but included large metro dailies as well: The *Contra Costa Times,* also owned at the time by Knight Ridder, ran a weekend real estate section written and paid for by developers but presented as news and *un*labeled as advertising;[60] The *Oakland Tribune,* owned by Dean Singleton's MediaNews Group (which bought all of Knight Ridder's Bay Area papers), ran "featurettes" praising various products and paid for by the product's manufacturer, without labeling them as advertising.[61] For the newspaper it was free content, including camera-ready photos and illustrations. MediaNews, one of the nation's largest chains, also ran real estate sections paid for and written by advertisers without being labeled as such. When we called them on it, they added an adverting tag in white ink and placed it illegibly on the white background of cover photos.[62] (Never underestimate the creativity of editors!) The *San Jose Mercury News*, ran ads formatted like news with microscopic advertising labels.[63] Other examples can be found at gradethenews.org.[64] In each case, editors eventually agreed to halt the deceptions, but some resumed the practice after Grade the News ceased active operation. All of these are instances of what University of Missouri Professor Glen T. Cameron calls "information pollution."[65]

Hidden advertising on TV news

James Rainey, a media reporter at the *Los Angeles Times*, described a similar covert practice in local television news:

> With summer ending, local television news stations recently rolled out their back-to-school features. In 10 big cities, that meant an appearance by a young mother and "toy expert" named Elizabeth Werner.

> Werner whipped through pitches for seven toys in just a few minutes. Perky and positive-plus, Werner seemed to wow morning news people in towns like Detroit, Atlanta and Phoenix. They oohed and aahed as they smelled Play-Doh, poked at mechanical bugs and strummed an electronic guitar she brought to the studio.

> Though parents might have welcomed the advice, and even bought some of the toys, they probably would have liked to know that Werner serves as a spokeswoman for hire, not an independent consumer advocate. She touted only products from companies that forked over $11,000 (the initial asking price, anyway) to be part of her back-to-school television "tour."

But viewers in several of the cities would have had no way of knowing that Werner's pitches amounted to paid advertising, because their local news stations failed to meet their legal obligation to identify the segments as paid promotions.

The practice goes way beyond Los Angeles and a product or two. Be warned if you are watching a self-proclaimed consumer advocate on local TV news pitching cars, electronics, travel and much more. There's a good chance that your friendly small-screen expert has taken cash to sell, sell, sell.[66]

Structural advertising influence

By far the most common type of advertiser influence, however, is even more subtle: editors choose story topics and assign "beats"[67] not based on citizens' information needs but in order to attract demographic groups advertisers hope to reach with their messages.[68] The news is structured for the benefit of advertisers.

This subordination of public interest to advertisers' interests leads to two abuses. First, sponsored topics — those that advertisers believe will channel attention to their ads — may get more attention than they deserve. Think of whole sections of the newspaper devoted to automobiles, real estate, food, entertainment, and travel. But topics that don't sell *products* —foreign affairs, religion, science (other than consumer technology), government, transportation, and social issues – get less attention than they merit. The second abuse is that those members of the community with the best "customer potential" for advertisers will have stories addressed to their interests. Those citizens less able or less inclined to buy will be less likely to have their information needs served. The Maynard Institute for Journalism Education has repeatedly drawn attention to large holes in news coverage corresponding to issues important to the urban poor.[69]

Letting corporate and government publicists supply the news

As repeated layoffs hollow out newsrooms, managers have been demanding that the remaining journalists produce more: more stories per week, more versions of those stories as reporters update newscasts, Web sites (including audio and video clips), and perhaps write a daily blog or curate an online discussion. Maybe even produce a stream of Twitter tweets. *New York Times* Public Editor Arthur S. Brisbane wrote: "For journalists charged with feeding the digital news flow, life is a barely sustainable cycle of reporting, blogging, tweeting, Facebooking and, in some cases, moderating the large volume of readers who comment online. I applaud these journalists for their commitment, but worry that the requirements of the digital age are translating into more errors and eventual burnout."[70]

Public relations agents can ease this overload by suggesting story ideas and supplying some or all of the "reporting." In his book about the British press, journalist Nick Davies calls this "churnalism" – "the rapid repackaging of largely unchecked second-hand material, much if it designed to service the political or commercial interests of those who provide it."[71]

'A shift of power from citizens to institutions'

Steven Waldman, author of the FCC's comprehensive two-year study of changes in the media, described a paradox: "One of the characteristics of the modern digital media era is it empowers people. [But] there's this countervailing trend, which basically is a shift of power from citizens to institutions — to government, to companies, because they're in a better position to drive the storyline."[72]

According to University of Florida Professor Spiro Kiousis, up to 70-80% of news stories in the U.S. originate either in a press release or contact with a publicist. It varies with the study and news media studied, he added. "It's safe to say half on a pretty consistent basis." News media reliance on public relations has grown over time, he explained, even before the Internet. "In recent years that reliance has increased for a couple of reasons: the newsroom layoffs have compounded that; plus the digital technologies that have created the 24/7 news cycle.

"The topics and emphasis present in public relations materials will be present in news content," he explained, "but you're very rarely going to see exact content, copied and pasted. The reality is that it's grabbed and repacked in some kind of news format." [73]

In local television news, such "information subsidies," to use University of Pennsylvania Professor Oscar Gandy's apt term, can include video news releases (VNRs) produced by corporations or governments. The video clips look like independent journalism, but promote the products or points of view of their sponsors. VNRs were aired at 69 stations, according to a study conducted by the Center for Media and Democracy's PRWatch.org.[74] Only two of those stations clearly identified the source of the material as public relations rather than independent reporting.

Outsourcing investigative reporting

Not only are corporations and government programming the journalist-depleted media, political Super Pacs have deployed legions of opposition researchers to dig up dirt on rival candidates and feed them to reporters who want scoops but don't have the time to sift through every historical vote and quote of political hopefuls. Joe Hagan, an investigative reporter for *Vanity Fair* and *New York Magazine* described the press' increasing reliance on political operatives in an interview on NPR's Fresh Air:

What these guys realize is that you can dig up all this negative information, but if it's coming from ... a Romney press release, let's say about Gingrich, it's going to have a lot less gravity with people than if it comes out in a newspaper like the *New York Times*, or it comes out on MSNBC or CNN, or what have you.

There are more of those opposition researchers, and there are maybe less of the reporters. So ... the power ... on the day-to-day reporting in the news cycle is with these opposition researchers.[75]

Politicians have always tried to entice reporters to investigate their opponents, but never on such a scale nor with so much information pre-reported. Why the change? In its 2010 "Citizens United" decision, the Supreme Court opened the door for "Super Pacs" — organizations loosely affiliated with candidates that are able to solicit unlimited political contributions from wealthy individuals, corporations and unions.

The obvious problem with public relations' enhanced role in journalism is that those special interests with deep enough pockets to hire publicists have the opportunity not only to set much of the news agenda for the community, but sometimes to write the news for the benefit of their clients. It saves the news organization money in discovering and reporting news, but at a cost to its ethically-mandated independence from those special interests. Groups without such resources become less "newsworthy." Not least, the public may be blind to the practice because it's usually hidden by news media trying to appear "objective."

Public relations content is socially valuable when it alerts journalists to legitimate stories and when it truthfully represents corporate or government viewpoints. But when strapped newsrooms rely heavily on PR agents to learn what's happening in the community or use press releases for anything more than one clearly attributed side of the story, they are participating in corporate and official propaganda rather than journalism. The watchdog that depends on the intruder for meals becomes a lap dog.

4. Commercial bias represents a greater threat to democracy than liberal or conservative bias

Commercialism is the most damaging bias in journalism because when it isn't distracting us from what matters, it's distorting reality. But news media rarely cover it, much less cop to it. No industry can be counted on to expose its flaws. Perhaps as a smokescreen, pundits are preoccupied instead with liberal or conservative political bias. But other than Fox, MSNBC, and the *Huffington Post*, most journalists work hard — and I think successfully — to avoid taking political sides.[76] Commercial bias, on the other hand, is as common as lobbyists on Capitol Hill.

Historically, the news business has guarded against the offenses of *individual* journalists. Plagiarism and conflicts of interest are routinely punished, often by firing. But *institutional* malpractice seems immune even from exposure. In fact, many executives excuse commercial bias, saying it has always been a part of news. But can you imagine the public outcry if doctors dismissed complaints of malpractice or if engineers shunned responsibility for collapsed bridges by pointing out that it's happened before?

Even more common is the argument by some news executives that if entertainment trumps information, the *public* is to blame for reading and watching such content, not the *media* for presenting it. Junk journalism is the *consumer's* fault. But when media skimp on expensive ways of attracting attention — investigative and enterprise reporting — and substitute cheap-to-report, entertaining articles to gather a crowd, is it appropriate to blame only the victim? Journalism aspires to be a profession as respected as law or medicine. But who would trust the doctor who tells patients what they want to hear rather than what's healthful? A dentist offering patients candy to ensure repeat business would become a laughingstock if he defended the practice by arguing that he was merely giving people what they want.

Don't get me wrong: Entertainment is an important part of any news capable of attracting a mass audience. But its task is to *serve* information — to make what's important interesting.

In terms of impact on a society that aims to govern itself, commercial bias corrodes civic engagement far more than the occasional act of plagiarism or a reporter's off-duty participation in an anti-war march. Systematically displacing substance with sensation, masking PR and advertising as independent journalism, and pitching the news at potential customers rather than at citizens cause far greater harm. Because it's covert, commercial bias creates a public that thinks it knows what's going on — because it pays attention to what news media highlight — but really doesn't. Thinking you know when you don't makes you vulnerable. You drop your guard. The majority in a society more entertained than informed by its news media can be manipulated by the powerful using skillful advertising and public relations. They've been set up.

As Walter Lippmann warned nearly a century ago, the weakest link in democracy has always been the limited willingness of the majority of people to do the real work of becoming informed, active citizens.[77] Economist Anthony Downs has argued that ignorance of civic affairs is, in fact, rational.[78] That's because individuals who can't afford lobbyists and major campaign contributions have so little influence over political outcomes – one vote among thousands, or at the national level, 100 million. Encouraging civic involvement and bracing that weak link is the purpose of socially responsible journalism. Chopping away at it by distracting people from the difficult issues of the day is not just irresponsible, it's antidemocratic. (There, I feel better now.)

Now that we've explored how institutional demands can interfere with public service, let's turn our attention to what the public can reasonably expect from news and other information-providers regardless of whether they act within an institution or on their own.

5

Setting Realistic Standards for Judging News and Information

I'm not a slave to objectivity. I'm never quite sure what it means. And it means different things to different people.

~ Peter Jennings, former ABC Evening News anchor

American journalism has long embraced an impossible, and I would argue, undesirable, standard — objectivity.

To see why, consider what a truly objective account of something — say a day in a typical American city — would look like. By definition, an objective view of something is one *unaffected by the viewer*. A biased view is the opposite — one influenced by the viewer, usually through the conscious or unconscious imposition of a set of values.[1] An objective account would capture the occurrences in a locality like a giant videocamera on autopilot. It would have to be a magic camera able to see through buildings. And able to capture what's going on below the earth's surface where oil, water, gas or magma is pooling, and the crust may be slipping.

In an objective account of a day's events, the story of each grass blade's growth — or its being cut down in the prime of life by a lawn mower — would be as important as a war or flood. To elevate one over the other would impose the observer's values on the account. Objective reporting would describe *everything* in the enhanced viewfinder of the giant camera, even the things that didn't change. It would be as exciting as watching a bank of surveillance cameras hour after hour. No one would want to consume truly objective news. Way too much information!

American journalism's preoccupation with objectivity has caused a heap of trouble. To see why and set out an alternative, this chapter will explore three propositions that apply to all of those purporting to tell us the truth, especially those claiming to provide news:

1. **Rather than eliminating bias, objectivity norms tend to hide it.**

2. **To be useful to society, news *must* be biased, but only in three ways: for the common good; for brevity; and for making what's important interesting.**

3. **Empiricism, not objectivity, should be the standard for presenting claims of fact.**

Let's begin with the first statement above. As practiced in many newsrooms, objectivity conventions have obstructed honest reporting and confused both journalists and the public. Here's how:

First, objectivity conveys false assurance that journalists see the world as it is — without any biases of their own. That's one reason the media were caught flat-footed when poor blacks rioted in America's inner cities in the 1960s. The commission studying the causes of those fiery disturbances concluded:

The media report and write from the standpoint of a white man's world. The ills of the ghetto, the difficulties of life there, the Negro's burning sense of grievance, are seldom conveyed. Slights and indignities are part of the Negro's daily life, and many of them come from what he now calls "the white press" – a press that repeatedly, if unconsciously, reflects the biases, the paternalism, the indifference of white America.[2]

Second, objectivity creates the misperception that news media "reflect" the world like a mirror. In actuality, a few fallible humans assemble a partial description of a tiny percentage of current events with carefully selected words, sounds, and images. Given the time pressures on reporters and the sheer volume of content they are expected to produce, errors and misplaced emphases are inevitable. Even the very best reporting is an incomplete and rough first draft of history. Journalism suffers the greatest distortion when the story encompasses simultaneous multiple events that are geographically spread apart, many conflicting stakeholders, the inability to access all sides, and a turbulent context in which disparate currents of history are colliding. This is most evident during a war, but applies to many other newsworthy occurrences.

> "I would like to see us say — over and over until the point has been made — that the newspaper that drops on your doorstep is a partial, hasty, incomplete, somewhat flawed and inaccurate rendering of some of the things we have heard about in the past 24 hours."[3]
>
> ~ The late *Washington Post* political columnist David Broder

Even when journalists are equipped with cameras, what becomes the news is the result of when and where they pointed them and what was included, rather than edited out, during a story's construction. But with dramatic images, urgent music and soaring slogans, news media promise us comprehensive, reliable coverage — "All the news that's fit to print" — as the *New York Times* proclaims. Walter Cronkite, perhaps the most trusted American journalist ever, used to end his 22-minute nightly newscast on CBS with a slogan he privately conceded was ludicrous, "And that's the way it is on..." (and he'd state the date). Off the air, Mr. Cronkite said this: "We fall far short of presenting all, or even a goodly part, of the news each day that a citizen would need to intelligently exercise his franchise in this democracy."[4]

Third, as Peter Jennings' quote at the top of the chapter suggests, even journalists who have sworn allegiance to objectivity can't agree on its definition. In a thoughtful essay about the concept, *Columbia Journalism Review* editor Brent Cunningham wrote, "Ask ten journalists what objectivity means and you'll get ten different answers."[5] A standard that nobody agrees on is as useless as a temperance advocate at a fraternity party.

Fourth, objectivity encourages reliance on official sources, even when reporters believe they are being spun or deceived. That's because it's much easier to report and defend the accuracy of *quotes* from designated authorities than to seek and defend the best version of the *truth* a journalist can obtain. But when the official view is considered an objective view, it gives voice mainly to the powerful. The poor and minorities often become invisible in such news, unless they break the law. And then their depiction contributes to a divisive stereotype. Objectivity invites journalistic passivity and official manipulation.

"The hallowed journalistic tradition of 'objectivity' often becomes confused with deference to authority and power."[6]

~ W. Lance Bennett, University of Washington media scholar.

Abandoning objectivity allows journalists to escape the passive observer's role, so that they can *advocate* for the public interest. They are empowered to ask the *public's* questions rather than waiting for officials to act or speak. Journalists are freed to prioritize the information needs of citizens above the publicity wants of sources.[7]

Fifth, objectivity pushes journalists toward creating a false balance — equal time or space — when two or more sides do not have equal evidence for their positions. You may personally doubt that human activity is warming the planet. But climate scientists have reached near unanimity that it is.[8] When journalists give the few climate-change deniers equal standing with the legion of scientists warning of serious environmental consequences, they enable obfuscation. They collaborate in confusing the public.

Finally, journalistic objectivity developed historically not so much as a means of pursuing truth, but for economic reasons. In the second half of the 19th century, as businessmen took over journalism from small printers and advertisers became the primary funders of news supplanting political parties, it became more profitable to report from a neutral position and gather as many readers as possible from across the political spectrum. The more readers, the more advertising dollars. Partisan reporting alienated potential customers. A neutral stance also greased access to officials from all parties. And it cut reporting costs, allowing the formation of press associations where a single reporter could cover an event impartially for many newspapers. Standing for nothing was a strategy aimed at getting along with everyone.[9]

If you're thinking what I think you're thinking, stop: Abandoning objectivity does *not* mean that journalists should give up trying to present accurate accounts of events and issues. If journalists don't restrain their individual subjectivity, society won't be able to agree on the nature of its problems or appropriate solutions. Further, accuracy matters *more* when news media investigate on behalf of the public than when they rely on government officials to investigate and merely report what the officials found. When journalists themselves uncover corruption or incompetence, they take full legal and moral responsibility. If they want to avoid lawsuits and public condemnation, they'd better get the facts right.

2. To be useful to society, news must be biased, but only in three ways: for the common good; for brevity; and for making what's important interesting

We want — and need — journalists to survey the great buzzing confusion of the world for us and do the laborious job *of picking out and pursuing what's most significant* for us to know. Further, we want them to *package it in interesting ways that invite us to care about the news.* And to *simplify it* so we can get the gist quickly. But each of these three processes introduces bias. Each requires subjective professional judgments. To my mind, these are necessary biases in a democracy. If we are overloaded with information without a hint as to which is most important, or if the presentation is boring or interminable, most of us shut down. Our impulse to become informed citizens is easily smothered.

The idea that news must be biased to be useful to a mass audience may sound radical. But most of journalism's codes of ethics have stated or implied a public service obligation both in news selection and presentation. They just haven't called it a bias because there's marketing value in the idea that journalists can be — and indeed are — value-free truth-tellers. Claiming to be bias-free allows one to reject any blame when what's reported upsets people. "Don't shoot the messenger!" we journalists shout. "We are neutral, merely reflecting reality."

The most important of these three positive biases is the first. Those events and issues that a community must understand to make wise collective and personal decisions should enjoy a clear preference over others — a bias for what matters. How well public schools are performing ought to trump how well the nearest professional sports team is faring. What might be done to make the community safer matters more than stories limited to an individual accident, fire or crime. Further, the way these consequential topics are reported ought to reflect a noticeable bias for the common good. Reporting should focus on what the public needs to know, rather than on what officials or corporations want them to know. In any public controversy, journalists should seek answers to this question: Which approach is most likely to generate the greatest benefit for the largest number, without compromising the basic rights of anyone?

The definition of the common good has been gradually expanded over two centuries in the United States. The Constitution promised every citizen "inalienable" rights to life, liberty, and the pursuit of happiness. But until the 20th century, most Americans were denied them. Only after long and painful struggle were African-American slaves, people without property or a certain level of education, and women permitted to vote and provided equal protection of laws. A bias for the common good embraces the well-being of all in the community. And all should be welcome to the public conversation defining it. That ongoing debate about the meaning of the common good in each community should be a central and recurring focus of both news and commentary. Rather than imposing their own views of what the community needs from on high, journalists should ground their daily decision-making in the public debate.[10]

The bias for brevity requires journalists to ignore many more issues and events than they cover. Even within a single story, they must prioritize, often leaving out more than they report. The winnowing process is guided by a value system, ensuring bias. But it's necessary because most Americans are too busy to surveil all of the day's relevant developments.

The bias for making what's important interesting acknowledges that we are not disembodied intelligences. We're not Vulcans like Mr. Spock. There's a little bit of Homer Simpson in all of us. We sometimes need the immediate reward of human interest, skilled story-telling, and evocative images to attract and hold our attention. Our flickering impulse to become informed citizens is as easily extinguished as a candle in the wind. Apathy is so much easier.

By arguing that news ought to contain three positive biases, I'm rejecting two characteristics commonly held up as journalistic ideals: neutrality and balance. I think news should always take the public's side, rather than taking an aloof, neutral stance. News providers should be independent, but not impartial. That means asking the public's questions and refusing to bow to pressures brought by special interests from within or without the newsroom. For example, local developers may insist that population growth and new subdivisions signify a prosperous community and media owners may agree, arguing that trees don't buy papers or watch newscasts. But journalists must ask who will gain and who will lose from such development, and what will be the effect on the overall environment and quality of life. As for balance, giving all sides a chance to make their case is important, but equalizing minutes or paragraphs devoted to competing positions makes sense only when the available evidence for alternative sides is roughly equal. Otherwise it's a false equivalence, a distortion of reality.

3. Empiricism, not objectivity, should be the standard for presenting claims of fact

In place of objectivity, anyone who provides us with information claiming to be factual should be held to a demanding but reachable standard — *empiricism*. It's a pursuit of truth based on dispassionate observation and logic. Here is what it requires of *anyone* providing news:

> 1. The quotes and personal observations are accurate. Someone tagging along with the reporter would see and hear the same things.

> 2. All fact-claims[11] are presented in context, including the full identification of the source of the claim, except in those circumstances where such identification might

realistically put the source at risk of harm. There is no attempt to exaggerate, tell half-truths or mislead.

3. The process of assembling facts into a narrative is rigorously logical, loyal only to the evidence and the public good, and free from undisclosed conflicts of interest.

4. Diverse perspectives from those most affected are included or at least sought.

5. All assertions of fact that are not based on either common knowledge or a reporter's direct observation are attributed to a trustworthy source. Further, claims of fact that are consequential are checked for accuracy, or — second-best — flagged as unconfirmed at the time of publication. When sources disagree, there's an attempt to triangulate toward truth by sources who are neutral and expert or experienced.

6. Finally, news providers humbly acknowledge that every account of reality is partial and subject to revision. Therefore, they promptly correct errors and omissions.

In the next chapter we'll apply these standards in what I call the SMELL test for bias.

6

The SMELL Test

Everybody is sitting around saying, 'Well, jeez, we need somebody to solve this problem of bias.' That somebody is us.

~ Wilma Mankiller, late Cherokee leader

Take a gander at this screenshot of a Web site called "Consumers News Reporting."

Are your teeth a little dingy? Maybe this is for you. To decide, it's useful to begin by asking what or who is the *source*

of this information? "Consumer News Reporting" sounds a lot like that magazine that rates products, *Consumer Reports*. And it carries the logos of ABC, CBS, CNN, MSNBC and *USA Today*, after the words "As seen on." Does that mean they have reported on "Mom's trick to whiter teeth"? The article is laid out like news with a headline, columns of text and (cute) photos, even what looks like a wire service identifier "(CNR)" at the beginning. Is "Consumer News Reporting" worthy of trust?

To find out, let's consider their *motivation*? Are they informing us about a cheap way to brighten our smile? Or trying to sell something? If the latter, we'd know to be very skeptical.

The story describes "Amy, a local school teacher and mom" who inexpensively whitened her teeth using a combination of "Bella Brite" and "Ortho White." The word "advertorial" appears in small and fainter type at the top of the page. It's an obscure trade term for advertising laid out like news but labeled as advertising. But this isn't clearly labeled. Scrolling down I noticed that you can buy the products right from the Web site, an unusual feature in a standard news story. And a discount was offered, but about to expire. That's a pressure sales tactic. It's beginning to look like an ad masquerading as news. But to be sure, let's look for more clues.

What *evidence* is offered to support the story's principal assertion? Well, there's a "before and after" photo: "Amy's Teeth Closeup." Sure enough, they're much whiter after. And there's Amy's testimony, plus that of man called "Jack." There's even a comment box. And all are recent, within 10 days of when I accessed the site. It looked like this:

Comments *(45 out of 45)*

Read Responses For: *"Don't Break the Bank: A Mom's Trick to Whiter Teeth"*

Johanna says: May 11, 2011 @Jack - those are amazing results! I just see that today the two promo codes will expire! I guess I was lucky to still get them. Everybody hurry up... :-)

Mike says: May 11, 2011 I smoked for quite a few years. recently quit and wanted to whiten my teeth, dentist quoted $450!!!!! this is great

Kevin says: May 11, 2011 Been a smoker all my life. My wife showed me this... We ordered both trials and had the same results as Jack. His photos say it all!!!

Does this evidence *logically* support the article's conclusion?

Forty-five comments were posted. All were wildly enthusiastic about the product. But how likely is that? Even sliced bread has its detractors (mostly French). Universal acclaim is more consistent with the sunny world of advertising than real life!

A final question: Is anything *left out*?

Since we're talking about changes to the human body, it would be nice to see at least one double-blind experiment testing the effectiveness of the product conducted by a university or independent lab. Or maybe a seal from the American Dental Association assuring us that it's both safe and effective. I scrolled to the bottom of the page to be sure I didn't miss anything.

Ten screens of gleaming teeth down, at the bottom of the page, I found a block of tiny gray type more than a screen deep written in legalese, under the heading "terms and services." It contained this disclaimer:

We are not affiliated in any way with CNN, WebTV, News Channel 7, ABC, NBC, MSNBC, CBS, U.S. News or FOX.

In the middle of the block it revealed that the site is operated by OrthoWhite and BellaProducts, which make the products it's "reporting" on. A clear conflict of interest. Then, at the very bottom I found the *coup de gras*:

> The story depicted on this site and the person depicted in the story are not real. Rather this stoty [sic] is based on the results that some people who have used these products have achieved. The results protrayed [sic] in the story and in the comments are illustrative and may not be the results that you achieve with these products. This page receives compensation for clicks on or purchase of products featured on this site.

The Consumer News Reporting site was obviously designed to mislead the unwary. It carried small type warnings as a fig leaf against prosecution by the Federal Trade Commission, which is supposed to protect consumers from fraudulent advertising. (I accessed the site in May, 2011. It has since been taken down, but similar sites abound. It also illustrates how deceitful content on the Web can be.) If all deceptive information providers were so obvious, you wouldn't need this book. But most bias is far more subtle. To reveal latent bias and distinguish more reliable information from less, we can use the same five questions asked above, which form an acronym — the SMELL test.

S is for **Source**. Who is providing the information? A traditional news outlet, a special interest group, a neighborhood blogger, the Ku Klux Klan? We'll be asking whether they know what they're talking about. And we'll be looking for conflicts between the source's self-interest and our interest in honest information. The presence of such a conflict doesn't invalidate the information, but it does alert us to a likely slant.

M is for **Motive**. Why is the source providing this information? Is it primarily designed to inform, persuade (including sell), or entertain? How can we tell?

E is for **Evidence.** What evidence is provided to support the thesis or gist of the story or message?

L is for **Logic.** Does the news or information make sense? Do the generalizations or conclusions follow from that evidence? Are they compatible with what we already know?

L is for **Left out.** What is missing either through ignorance or intention? Which relevant facts or stakeholders are absent or marginalized? What *alternative* conclusions might the facts support?

Information can be unreliable for three reasons: because it's deliberately biased, unintentionally biased, or simply inaccurate. Intentional bias is usually carefully hidden. Like a python draped on a tree in the jungle, it depends for its effectiveness on camouflage. Unintentional biases, in contrast, are so deeply embedded in our way of seeing the world that we don't notice them even though they lie in plain sight. We take them for granted as true or natural, the way that a thousand years ago most humans believed in a flat earth, or the way that only a hundred years ago federal law considered women unfit to vote. Information also can be unreliable due to simple ignorance, or either inability or failure to check it out.

Not long ago, many of us could rely on the natural enemy of bias and ignorance — robust professional journalism. As such journalism recedes, however, we need to learn how to spot unreliable information ourselves and warn others. We need to become information *detectives*, taking a magnifying glass at least to those messages that most affect our well-being.

S: Who is the *Source* of the information?

The simplest case is when *individuals*, perhaps colleagues at school or at work, provide information about something they have witnessed. But usually there are at least two levels of sources: immediate — the person speaking, and secondary — the source(s) of his/er information, e.g., heard it from a friend, read it in a book, saw it on TV, etc.

Information we learn directly from *institutions*, e.g., Web sites or other media, typically has three levels of sources: 1) the organization itself; 2) the author whose name is on the article; and 3) the source or sources the author relied on for raw material. Add a fourth if a friend tells us about something seen on TV or the Web.

Each layer acts as a filter. Each alters the information for its own purposes and in accord with its own biases. The more links in the information chain, the more opportunity for distortion. (Remember the telephone game where one person whispers a message to another and by the end of the chain, it's unintelligible?) So, whenever possible, it's a good idea to go directly to the source closest to the original event. As a practical matter, that's often a media outlet.

To keep things simple, we can usually combine the author and organization levels when the information provider is an institution such as a media company. As we saw in chapter four, most authors work with editors and colleagues and all must comply with standards set by the owner. Those standards are enforced because the institution's reputation and freedom from law suits are at risk regardless of which employee authors the information. So often we can streamline our analysis to two layers — the institution providing the news or information and the sources quoted within the article.[1]

"As anyone in the business will tell you, the standards and culture of a journalistic institution are set from the top down, by its owner, publisher and top editors."[2]

~ Carl Bernstein, investigative reporter and author

Let's begin our credibility audit with the immediate level — the individual or institution providing the information. It's convenient to judge the reliability of a provider by reputation: "Marcy has never lied to me before," or "The *Washington Post* has a reputation for accuracy." That's a valuable shortcut when we know the source well. But there's another way that's less vulnerable to our own blind spots. Whether it's an individual friend or colleague, a Web site such as Gawker or the Drudge Report, or a national organization, such as NBC News or the *New York Times,* all sources can be judged on three logical criteria, which form the acronym PIE:

> 1. *Proximity* to the event or whatever information is provided. Was the source an eye- or ear-witnesses with unobstructed access? For information, was the source in a position to know first-hand? Or is the information hearsay passed on from others? When the provider is an institution, such as a news organization, we can ask whether its agent or reporter — or better, multiple reporters — were able to observe events for themselves? The closer the source to the action and the less occluded the view, the better our chances for reliable information.

> 2. *Independence*, or freedom from conflict of interest. Does the source stand to gain from telling the story, or describing it in a particular way? Self-interest is such a powerful perception-bender that we're always wise to discount information for any advantage it may generate for the source.

> 3. *Expertise* or lived *Experience*. Is the source knowledgeable, having studied, supervised or had prolonged experience that would lend confidence to his/er report? For news media and other institutional information providers, does their agent have specialized knowledge, e.g. a reporter covering courts who has a law degree, or long experience covering the subject?

If we don't want to be fooled, the higher our information provider ranks on these three criteria the better. If our informant is relying on others, e.g. a reporter building a story from interviewing sources, it's essential to evaluate the sources s/he relied on as well.

Assessing the credibility of the information-providers' sources

Given that "Amy," the primary source in the teeth-whitening article, was fictional, it's important to apply our PIE criteria to sources quoted *within* a particular message or news account. Credible information will *always* include the sources who provided it, identified by position and usually by name. Only sources who would suffer harm from being named should be permitted anonymity, and even these should be identified by position.[3] These identifiers are necessary to help us recognize their biases and decide how much to believe of what the source says. They also get the source on the record, creating accountability. (People speaking with full attribution are normally more careful about their comments than those permitted anonymity. That's why we should always give greater credence to named sources.) Given that the reliability of information depends on its source, it's useful to map sources on the following matrix, at least in our minds:

Assessing Source Credibility – The PIE Chart			
	Low	Medium	High
Proximity			
Independence			
Expertise			

Assign each identified source in the message or story a number based on the order in which they first appear in the story. Then place that number in the appropriate box for each of the three credibility criteria. If the first source mentioned is high in proximity and independence, but low in expertise, we'd put a 1 in each of the three appropriate boxes. Documentary sources — books, reports, memos, etc. — can be classified by their author(s)' placement on the grid. The greater the number of sources, the more diverse their backgrounds, and the more they fall to the right in the matrix, the more trustworthy the story. Diversity is useful because, as we saw in chapter three, people see the same thing differently depending on their self-interest and across social "fault lines" of race, class, gender, etc.

Applying the criteria

Suppose you want to know how safe the childhood vaccines most public schools require really are. You put the term "childhood vaccine safety" in Google or other search engine. In April 2011, I got 242,000 results from Google. I noticed the third and fourth entries on the first results page both came from the "cdc.gov" Web site, the Centers for Disease Control in Atlanta, which is run by the federal government. As they have the resources to study the issue first-hand, information from that site would rate high in **P**roximity. Also in **E**xpertise, given that physicians and other highly trained specialists conduct the research. Finally, the CDC has no stake in selling vaccines, but is supposed to have a stake in public health; improving it is their mission. The agency is **I**ndependent. Sometimes government regulators are captured by the industries they are supposed to oversee, but absent evidence to the contrary, I would rate the CDC Web site high on all three criteria.

The eighth search result, midway down the first page, came from "Shirley's Wellness Cafe" (shirleys-wellness-cafe.com). The lead article on the site was headlined: "Vaccination – Deception and Tragedy." As both descriptors are negative, the headline signals a one-sided exploration of the topic. Clicking on the "about Shirley" link to investigate the source's qualifications led me to her biography, which began:

> I was once a victim of the never-ending flow of propaganda from the medical establishment (which I think of as the "disease" establishment because they focus on disease rather than on prevention and wellness) who wants to maintain a monopoly on the word "cure" and who wants us to believe that we have no control over our own health and that our only hope to get "well" is with drugs, surgery and radiation. Below is my account about how I achieved optimum health without drugs, surgery or radiation.[4]

Shirley Lipschutz-Robinson claims to be the proprietor of the site. She appears to be a well-meaning crusader for homeopathic and alternative remedies. She claims no medical education, nor research beyond anecdotes of her own experiences and several others, but speaks of the wonders of "glutathion, therapeutic clays, fulvic minerals and shilajit, Himalayan crystal salt, marine phytoplankton, wheatgrass juice, tonic herbal extracts, herbal teas, and the unique immune support of Transfer Factor." She rejects traditional medicine.

It's unclear how the site is funded, but she praises a variety of books and remedies and provides links to purchase them. None are labeled as advertisements, so we don't know the site's sponsors.

As a source of information about childhood vaccines, I would rate her low in **P**roximity and **E**xpertise. Her **I**ndependence is difficult to determine from the Web site. Skepticism is always the default for sources of information that don't list their major sources of income (assuming it's not obvious from advertisements, subscription fees, or government funding). So I would rate the site low here as well.

Given these results, we should analyze the secondary sources *within* Ms. Lipschutz-Robinson's article with our shields raised.

Analyzing the secondary sources turns out to be challenging because of the article's unusual organization. Rather than an essay, it's a collection of 133 snippets. Most are quotations ranging from a sentence to several paragraphs long by various authors, only a few of whom are medical doctors. Most blurbs contain links to articles elsewhere on the Web. A significant minority of the entries appear to be blurbs praising books damning vaccinations of all sorts. All but one of the snippets condemn vaccination. The exception was a 2010 Frontline special called The Vaccine War,[5] but it was criticized on Shirley's Wellness Cafe' for failing to include homeopathic alternatives to vaccination.

It was too burdensome to map all the blurbs and their links, so I chose those that seemed most authoritative. One was a YouTube video featuring environmental activist Robert F. Kennedy Jr. charging that the federal CDC had conspired with large pharmaceutical companies to hide the dangerous side effects of common children's vaccines preserved with thimerosal, a mercury-based compound once common in vaccines. Checking on the video's authenticity, I entered "Robert F. Kennedy Jr." and "childhood vaccines" together in Google. I quickly learned that he made similar claims in a 2005 article, "Deadly Immunity," jointly published by Salon.com and *Rolling Stone Magazine*. I also noticed that in January 2011, Salon took the article down from its Web site claiming serious factual errors.[6] *Rolling Stone* also deleted the article from its online archive. Because it involves eating crow, publishers disavow articles very infrequently. This raised my suspicions.

A second blurb on the Wellness Web site credited an English physician, Andrew Wakefield, whose research on the link between vaccines and autism had been published in a prominent medical journal. Googling "Andrew Wakefield," I was able to learn that the *British Medical Journal* had retracted his article and accused him of an elaborate fraud. Dr. Wakefield's article had been the only published scientific research connecting autism with children's vaccines, a worrying sign in itself (that we'll explore ahead when we talk about logic).

The most recent blurb at Shirley's Wellness Cafe was the April, 2010 PBS Frontline report. I chose it because it was the most up-to-date reference (knowledge changes over time) and because of Frontline's reputation for quality journalism. The report concluded that the largest, best-designed research showed no connection between standard childhood vaccines and autism.

With the three sources that seemed most authoritative all showing a consistent pattern, I decided against believing Ms. Lipschutz-Robinson's reports and can't recommend her Web site.

Google search rankings do not assess information quality

This comparison of sources' credibility was intended only as an example, but it shows something else that's important if we are to avoid being fooled: Google rankings are based on a proprietary algorithm (a one-size-fits-all set of computer instructions), *not* on any human assessment of the reliability of the information provided on sites.[7] Just because a source appears on the first page of search results, doesn't mean it's trustworthy.

When you can't identify the source

The PIE (Proximity, Independence and Expertise/ Experience) criteria are well and good, but what if you can't identify the source? Or it has a vague name wrapped in stars and stripes, like "Citizens for American Progress"?

Legitimate information sources will *always* disclose who they are. On the Web, they will have an "about us" link. If the producer of the content isn't identified, or seems at all coy about describing him/er/itself, believe *nothing* from it. The primary reason an information-provider — whether on a Web site or online video or in a viral email — chooses not to identify, or to mis-identify, itself is to disarm the audience. *Deception automatically invalidates content.* Treat such sites or email messages like poison ivy. Even if you're itching to, don't enable contagion by forwarding.

To evaluate independence from conflicts of interest — the I in PIE — you'll need to know who sponsors the information provider — the major donors. Unless it's obvious, Web sites and other media providing news and information should always state who pays the bills. If this information is not volunteered, ask before you trust. If the source draws support from advertisers, pay attention to the goods and services in the ads and compare them to the information provided. The greater the similarity between ads and content, the less trust you should repose in the information. Rational advertisers rarely pay to be placed in a critical environment.

If the information source is unfamiliar, investigate it by entering the name in Google or another search engine. Don't trust any sources you haven't vetted to discover their qualifications and sponsorship. Political influence groups, industry trade associations, and some think tanks have been known to adopt misleading names to disguise their self-interest. Consider the Foundation for Lung Cancer: Early Detection, Prevention & Treatment. Who could wear a whiter hat – or lab coat? But the *New York Times* discovered that the foundation was covertly underwritten almost entirely by the parent company of Liggett, a major cigarette maker.[8] In a 2010 story about the massive recall of eggs possibly tainted by salmonella, the *Washington Post* Web site added what it thought was a helpful link to a site called the Egg Safety Center (www.eggsafety.org). To the *Post's* embarrassment, the site turned out to be run by a PR firm for the United Egg Producers rather than a source of impartial expertise.[9] Even professional journalists need to look beyond that innocent or patriotic name.

M: What appears to be the information provider's *Motivation*?

Has the source gathered our eyeballs primarily to inform, persuade, or entertain? It's often unclear. There's money to be made and influence to be had by cloaking the source's intent.

Governments and corporations produce content that appears purely informational: oil companies so devoted to environmentalism they portray themselves as jolly green giants; banks lending a helping hand simply to prosper the community; and potential soldiers promised that they can somehow "be all that [they] can be," if they volunteer for an organization that will train them to kill.

Advertisers often pressure news organizations to present commercial messages as news because audiences may grant them greater credibility than they would an ad. Media managers may push journalists to provide "infotainment" in the guise of news, because it enlarges the audience.

To avoid being fooled, it's useful to learn the characteristics that reveal motivation.

The most obvious tip-off to a source's motivation is the tone established in the content, including images and sound. Trust your instinct. If it *feels* like the real intent is to persuade, or provoke a laugh or sigh, it probably is. Here are the characteristics of content primarily designed to inform, to persuade and to entertain.

Content designed to inform

Informers follow the rules of empiricism stated at the close of chapter 5. They stress established facts and careful, specific observation. Every assertion of fact that's not based on common knowledge or the author's direct observation is attributed to a source fully enough for the audience to apply the PIE test.

Informers practice fairness — dispassionately presenting all relevant sides to an issue in a context that aids audience understanding. No cherry-picking of facts to favor one side over another. Informers are careful to include the perspectives of all major parties with something at stake in the issue or event reported.

Informers are faithful to evidence rather than ideology (a unified way of interpreting issues and events, e.g. conservative, liberal). Informers prefer nuance (shades of gray) over black and white because life rarely demonstrates such sharp contrasts. They employ short, logical inferences to reach their conclusions. They avoid sweeping generalizations. They practice transparency (explaining how they know what they claim to know and warning about what they don't). The format is descriptive rather than argumentative. Except possibly for empathy, the presentation is unemotional (anger, fear, titillation, all retard reason). No judgment of right or wrong is proffered. No action is called for. Other than being concerned, you get the impression that the source cares little about what conclusion you draw or how you behave in response to the information. Photos and videos are used to document the text. They are neither choreographed nor posed. Natural sound predominates. Music is rare.[10]

These, by the way, are the standards of empirical reporting and what the best news organizations mean by objectivity.

Content designed to persuade

Because life is complicated and we're busy people, society also gains from principled persuasion that simplifies and explains. Persuasion is principled if it is: 1) true to the relevant facts, rather than manipulating or distorting them; 2) logical in that the evidence provided supports the conclusions drawn; and 3) transparent — content is labeled as opinion or commentary with the author fully identified so we can assess his/er proximity, independence and expertise/experience.

> Opinion writers "are not entitled to get the facts wrong or to so mangle them that they present a false picture,"[11]
>
> ~ Clark Hoyt, former public editor of the *New York Times*

During the 2012 Republican presidential primaries *New York Times* op-ed columnist Gail Collins repeatedly stretched Clark Hoyt's standard in describing a 1983 incident in which candidate Mitt Romney put the family's Irish setter, Seamus, in a wind-sheltered portable kennel on the roof of the family station wagon on a summer vacation trip to Canada. Even in a column devoted to Newt Gingrich's legacy, Ms. Collins couldn't resist writing that "Mitt Romney drove to Canada with the family Irish setter strapped on the car roof."[12] This was after fact-finding Web site PolitiFact, cited Ms. Collins for mentioning the incident in 17 previous columns.[13] By implying that the dog was tied to the roof without protection, the anecdote manipulates the truth to make Mr. Romney seem inhumane. (I realize I may have lost some dog-lovers here.)

Principled persuasion

Principled persuasion usually takes the form of an argument for a particular view of something: Where informers lay out the relevant facts and let readers or viewers decide what they mean, interpreters provide a preferred meaning. They often make judgments. Sometimes they call for action. Persuaders often apply an overarching ideology — perhaps pragmatic, liberal, conservative or libertarian — to create a simplified and coherent explanation of events and issues. But there is no attempt to disguise it.

If there is debate, it is civilized and respectful: No name-calling, personal attacks, taunts, shouting, or making fun of opposing persons or positions. There can be disagreement, but all sides listen to the others rather than talking over them.

Images and sound are generally similar to those produced when the purpose is to inform.

Unprincipled persuasion

Unprincipled persuasion involves some type of deceptive manipulation of the information presented or lack of care with fact claims. The tone is often emotional rather than logical. In broadcasts, conflict is common, because as the TV ringmaster Jerry Springer knows, it attracts an audience. In their smart book about intentional bias in messages, *UnSpun*, Brooks Jackson and Kathleen Hall Jamieson warn specifically about efforts to shut off thinking by arousing primal emotions. "If it's scary," they write, "be wary."[14] I'd add: "If they shout, tune it out."

Look for slogans and catch phrases such as "death taxes," "common sense solution," "socialist," "one-percenters" or "fat cats" which are often tested in focus groups for how they play on the ears of target audiences. Images are usually highly produced, sometimes digitally enhanced and chosen to provoke a specific reaction. They may significantly distort what they purport to describe. Music is sometimes played over words and images to heighten the emotional impact, much as it might be in a motion picture. If you've ever watched a political ad, you know it can be a potent brew.

Content designed to entertain

An entertainer may, but need not, adhere to facts. Logic, evidence, and fairness matter little. Exaggeration, even absurdity, are common. Emotion, however, is essential. To be successful, entertainment has to move you, even if it's just a smile or cringe. Dramatic images and music are carefully selected and sequenced.

It's tempting to overlook entertainment as a motivation because its primary function is to enthrall us and what it describes is often openly fictitious. But as the English social philosopher/nanny Mary Poppins observed, "a spoonful of sugar makes the medicine go down." Entertainment can leap-frog our rational faculties to exert powerful social effects, including fooling us.

Lauren Feldman, a communication professor at American University explained: "When audiences are exposed to political humor or satire, they are less likely to oppose the information in the message or question whether it is fair or accurate. Ultimately, it can affect the perceptions of a candidate."[15]

Satirists such as Tina Fey of Saturday Night Live, Jon Stewart and Stephen Colbert of Comedy Central, cartoonist Gary Trudeau and Bill Maher of HBO have understood as well as did Aristophanes and Jonathan Swift that humor can be uniquely persuasive. It can disarm our skepticism like a woman panhandling with a baby in her arms.

> "People remember Gerald Ford through the prism of Chevy Chase. Ford was among our most athletic presidents, and he had a wide-ranging knowledge of public-policy issues. But because of 'SNL,' many came to think of him as a buffoon."[16]
>
> ~ John Pitney Jr., professor of American politics at Claremont College.

According to Professor Feldman, Tina Fey's impression of then Republican vice-presidential candidate Sarah Palin hurt the McCain-Palin ticket. It earned SNL its highest overnight ratings in 14 years. And her impersonations became the most viewed videos on NBC's Web site during the election year. Millions more watched them on YouTube and Hulu.com. CNN began referring to them as the "Tina Fey effect," and speculated that Ms. Fey's version of Ms. Palin became confused in voters' minds with the real candidate.[17] But Saturday Night Live is not a news show. It exaggerated Ms. Palin's mannerisms and halting interview with CBS' Katie Couric.

Many young people claim to get much of their news from The Daily Show or The Colbert Report, but these too take liberties with the facts to make a joke. Mr. Stewart and Mr. Colbert openly proclaim themselves "fake journalists." You may learn something from such shows, especially when Mr. Stewart shows video clips of politicians contradicting themselves or Mr. Colbert demonstrates the absurdity of allowing unrestricted political contributions. But on Comedy Central the first rule is "make 'em laugh." Indeed, in April 2010, Mr. Stewart remarked: "I have not moved out of the comedian's box into the news box. The news box is moving towards me."[18]

Novels, plays, motion pictures, and cartoons often inform and persuade as well as entertain. Prior to the American Civil War, Harriet Beecher's Stowe's widely read account of the brutality of slavery in *Uncle Tom's Cabin* made the practice real — and repugnant — to Northerners. In 1862, Ms. Stowe met President Abraham Lincoln who reportedly quipped, "So you're the little woman who wrote the book that started this Great War!"[19] American Studies Professor David S. Reynolds called it "the most influential novel in American history and a catalyst for radical change both at home and abroad."[20]

To avoid being fooled, it's useful to subject satire and fiction to a modified version of the same criteria used for establishing the reliability of news and other information presented as factual. Even if the characters and setting are fictional, do they fairly illustrate the reality they purport to describe? We can ask, for example, how Ms. Stowe learned about plantation life (by looking at her online biography). Was she free of conflicts of interest? Was her primary purpose to entertain or inform, or to persuade? We can also apply the remainder of the SMELL test.

Infotainment

Just as a sugar coating of entertainment can make information appealing or mask persuasion, a veneer of information can mislead us to think we're keeping up with current affairs, when in fact we're merely being amused.

Beware of entertainment posing as news — stories designed to turn, but not fill, your head. The danger here is not so much that the latest misadventure of a spoiled celebrity, a distant, isolated act of violence, or the promotion of professional sports will be factually incorrect. The concern is that when the news is chosen and reported primarily to attract as much saleable attention as possible, it becomes a weapon of mass distraction.[21] As Jon Stewart observed, "The press can hold its magnifying glass up to our problems, bringing them into focus, illuminating issues heretofore unseen. Or they can use that magnifying glass to light ants on fire. And then perhaps host a week of shows on the sudden, dangerous flaming ant epidemic."[22]

Infotainment can be disrobed by asking: Regardless of how compelling — sexy, strange, amusing, visual, violent, or conflictual — it may be, how much does this information help me in making sense of the world around me? How much have I *learned* from it that I *needed* to know?

Politicians, who live in a tornado alley of spin, are fond of saying "if it walks like a duck and quacks like a duck, it is a duck." Regardless of how news and information sources label themselves, classify them for yourself on which set of characteristics best fit them. Be skeptical of all motivations but informing and principled persuasion.

E: What *Evidence* is provided to support the thesis or gist of the story or message?

Some information providers possess the confidence of the Framers of the Constitution: They believe what they assert as true to be self-evident. They make naked assertions, offered as if there is no need to attribute a claim of fact to an authoritative source, nor to assemble evidence for generalizations.

When providers offer no source or evidence for their claims, we have no choice but to fall back on our assessment of the provider's own credibility and, if mediated, the reputation of the institution on whose pages, airwaves or Web site the information appears. A distinguished professor writing within his/er expertise for a news outlet that forbids conflicts of interest and checks facts may merit trust, but we should be skeptical of less qualified information providers, particularly if they are working outside of institutions with a reputation for integrity. As a former journalist whose wary editors warned "if your mother says she loves you, check it out," I encourage you to be uncomfortable with the "trust me" school of evidence.

How do you know that?

To avoid being fooled whenever we hear an assertion about what's real or true, we should ask: *How do you know that?*

"I heard it on the grapevine" won't do. There are only three adequate answers: 1) I witnessed it; 2) I learned it from one or more sources (documentary or human) who rank high on the PIE source reliability matrix described earlier; 3) It logically follows from information provided in answers 1 or 2.

Trustworthy information providers should attempt to *confirm* or *verify* at least the most consequential or controversial claims of their sources. Verification means finding at least one other source, independent of the first and with a strong PIE score, who provides a similar description of an event. It's irresponsible to just hand over the megaphone of the media even to prominent sources — *especially* to prominent sources — enabling them to broadcast misinformation. Verification has become even more essential in our present sharply partisan political environment where candidates' spinning is as constant as their grinning and once something is posted on the Web it can metastasize at fiber optic velocity.

Obama's '$200 million a day' trip

On Nov. 4, 2010, CNN's Anderson Cooper provided a textbook example of verification. The night before he had interviewed Minnesota Republican Congresswoman Michele Bachmann about where Republicans proposed to cut spending for Medicare and Social Security. Dodging the question, Rep. Bachmann responded: "I think we know that just within a day or so the president of the United States will be taking a trip over to India that is expected to cost the taxpayers $200 million a day. He's taking 2,000 people with him. He'll be renting over 870 rooms in India, and these are five-star hotel rooms at the Taj Mahal Palace Hotel. This is the kind of over-the-top spending. It's a very small example.... " When Mr. Cooper asked the congresswoman how she knew this, she said she'd seen it in the news media.

Performing his own SMELL test, Mr. Cooper traced the first mention of the $200 million per day figure on the Web to an Indian wire service story. It quoted an unnamed bureaucrat from the Indian province of Maharashtra. "It was an anonymous quote," said Mr. Cooper. "Some reporter in India wrote this article with this figure in it. No proof was given; no follow-up reporting was done." Assuming such a source is real, s/he would score exceedingly low on proximity to the information and on expertise about U.S. presidential travel expenses, which even the White House doesn't divulge for security reasons. The Indian article was picked up in the U.S. on the Drudge Report, a conservative-leaning gossip Web site. From there it was treated as fact in scathing attacks on President Obama by Rush Limbaugh, Glenn Beck, Fox Business.com's Imus in the Morning, and Michael Savage. Mr. Cooper provided video clips of each.

He then showed White House and Pentagon spokesmen rejecting the figure, which totaled almost $2 billion over the nine-day, four-country visit, as vastly overstated. Mr. Obama's Press Secretary Robert Gibbs said, "Costs are comparable to when President Clinton and President Bush travelled abroad.

This trip doesn't cost $200 million a day." Pentagon spokesman Geoff Morrell called the report "just comical."

Mr. Cooper noted that the Congressional Budget Office estimated the cost of the entire war effort in Afghanistan at $190 million a day. "So the idea that a president's trip might cost more than the war in Afghanistan? That just doesn't make any sense." President Clinton's 1998 trip to Africa — with 1,300 people and of roughly similar duration, cost about $5.2 million a day in 2010 dollars, according to the Government Accountability Office, Mr. Cooper said. He concluded: "The guy from the Pentagon you saw earlier described this as 'comical.' Well it would be comical if it wasn't being used by a powerful congresswoman and powerful pundits."[23]

The decline of verification

Partisan pundits and politicians have been emboldened by changes in news media. At the close of 2009 and beginning of 2010, the Project for Excellence in Journalism surveyed mainstream news executives. One key finding: six in ten said the Internet is changing the fundamental values of journalism. "And their biggest concern is loosening standards of accuracy and verification, much if it tied to the immediacy of the Web." One broadcast executive wrote: "I worry that journalistic standards are dropping in that blogging and celebrity gossip and Tweets are being confused with reporting and editing that passes a rigorous standard."[24]

It takes time to find and interview reliable sources; even more time to check their fact-claims. Plus, their responses lengthen and complicate news reports. And all those attributions — "according to Jones," "Smith said," "Adams responded" — slow the reader or listener down. Given the understaffed, constant-deadline, multi-media newsrooms of the early 21st century, it's more important than ever for us to ask: "How do you know that?" of our news and information sources and to map the sources they quote on the PIE chart.

The nature of photographic and video evidence

Before the era of digital recording of images and software such as Photoshop that allows it to be completely altered so seamlessly that it is difficult to detect, photos and film were seen as the gold standard of evidence. Cameras, we said, don't lie. They capture reality without bias. And they don't forget.

The apparent unblinking objectivity of cameras was always an illusion, however. Even in the old days when news photographers wore bandoliers of spooled film cartridges, they often posed their subjects to make the images more dramatic. But the subjectivity of image creation is even more basic. Anyone who has pointed a camera knows that the images captured show only what's in focus within the lens at a given moment. Left unseen is everything that happened before and after the picture or the video clip was shot and everything that happened in other directions and locations. Editing narrows and manipulates this thin slice of reality even further. "Images are always mediated, and those who choose the angles, shots, et cetera, shape our perceptions," according to Arthur Asa Berger, a professor of visual communication at San Francisco State University.[25] Seeing should *not* lead to believing. More on this in chapter 7.

L: Does the evidence *Logically* support the conclusions drawn?

The fundamental question here is "Does this make sense?" and we can profitably ask it at two levels: 1) Externally — "Does this make sense in light of everything else I know?" (as Anderson Cooper did) and 2) Internally — "Is the evidence provided *within* the report adequate to support the conclusions reached?"

Obviously, the more you know, the better your answer to the first question will be. (Assuming what you know is correct.) That's why it's important to keep up with news from reliable sources. Information that jars you, that's "too good to be true," is particularly suspect. It requires an especially rigorous approach to question two about its internal logic.

Dissonant information puts us on alert. But we are most easily fooled when the answer to question one about whether the new information squares with the old is either "yes" or "I don't know." Because of this vulnerability, we can't stop with question one. For news or information that really matters we have to examine the internal logic.

Common media logic failures

Whole books are devoted to logic. Here I want to focus just on seven inter-related reasoning fallacies and failures of due diligence common to news and information providers.

1. Non-sequiturs: derive from a Latin phrase meaning "it doesn't follow." On Sept. 14, 2003, after U.S. and British forces had routed the Iraqi army, Vice President Dick Cheney said on NBC's Meet the Press: "If we're successful in Iraq ... so that it's not a safe haven for terrorists, now we will have struck a major blow right at the heart of the base, if you will, the geographic base of the terrorists who have had us under assault now for many years, but most especially on 9/11."[26] The conclusion that the U.S. will have "struck a major blow" at the "geographic base of the terrorists" who attacked the nation in 2001 by defeating the Iraqi resistance makes no sense if those terrorists attacked us from somewhere else, such as Afghanistan. When Mr. Cheney spoke to Meet the Press, it was already clear that Saddam Hussein's government had no connection with Al Qaeda nor Osama bin Laden, who launched the 9/11 terror attacks.[27]

In similar fashion, the administration had argued in 2002 that Iraq's purchase of high strength aluminum tubes necessarily led to the conclusion that the country was using them to process uranium into nuclear weapons. It turned out that there were other uses for aluminum tubes, such as rocket casings. But that leap of logic made the front page of *The New*

York Times on September 8, in a story quoting only anonymous sources.[28]

The way to recognize non-sequiturs is to convert a fact claim, perhaps the premise of a news report, into a syllogism: If A is true and B is true, therefore C must be true. Iraq has purchased thousands of aluminum tubes; one possible use of such tubes is to build centrifuges for purifying uranium to bomb level. Therefore Iraq is building a nuclear bomb. C doesn't necessarily follow from A and B.

In both of these examples, the source committed a non-sequitur error. Because journalists often fail to point out the illogic of their sources, we have to evaluate them ourselves to avoid being fooled. Also be careful not to accept without checking that A or B is true. President Bill Clinton based his defense against claims of an affair with White House intern Monica Lewinsky — "I did not have sex with that woman" — on the deceptive premise that "having sex" requires intercourse.

2. Overgeneralizations: Conclusions should stretch over evidence as tightly as a swimming cap covers an expensive hairdo. There should be little room for doubt to seep in. The evidence presented, plus common knowledge, should compel you to accept the information provider's conclusion. The broader the conclusion, the more evidence required.

A frequent type of overgeneralization occurs when anecdotes are presented as proof of something larger. Anecdotes are personal stories — vignettes — that providers properly use to add human interest to their articles. But a series of anecdotes doesn't prove anything, no matter how poignant they may be. They are merely a few data points that might easily be contradicted by other personal accounts the information provider didn't have — or take — time to gather.

So a news report in which several teachers tell vivid personal stories about students today failing to take school as seriously as young people did 20 years ago doesn't mean that the current generation is less engaged, nor even that teachers agree on this. Had the provider interviewed other teachers, s/he might have reported just the opposite conclusion. Neither would have been logical. *Only a sample where every member of a group has an equal opportunity to be included and the number interviewed represents a majority or a number large enough to allow statistical tests of significance can support generalizations about that group.*[29]

Beware of any generalizations or assertions that are not based on *systematic* evidence-gathering. Otherwise you may fall prey to examples cherry-picked from among contradictory cases to make a point.

Sweeping generalizations go hand-in-hand with imprecise quantifiers like "many," "largely," "a lot," "somewhat" and "up to (some number)." But how many is "many" or "a lot?" "Many" indicates number, not a proportion; it may not come close to a majority. How much is "somewhat?" "Up to" includes every number below it. Such words should alert us to a lack of definite facts or numbers, information that's incomplete if not misleading.

3. Innuendo: Information providers use innuendo when they want to leave an impression that's stronger than their facts can support. Innuendo implies something is true without stating it outright. It's what you read between the lines. If the author cannot state something plainly, ask yourself *why* it cannot be said explicitly. It could provide evidence of bias for or against the target of the leading statements.

On Feb. 21, 2008, the *New York Times* published a lengthy front-page article under the headline, "For McCain, self-confidence on ethics poses its own risk." Here's how the story began:

> WASHINGTON — Early in Senator John McCain's first run for the White House eight years ago, waves of anxiety swept through his small circle of advisers.

A female lobbyist had been turning up with him at fund-raisers, visiting his offices and accompanying him on a client's corporate jet. Convinced the relationship had become romantic, some of his top advisers intervened to protect the candidate from himself — instructing staff members to block the woman's access, privately warning her away and repeatedly confronting him, several people involved in the campaign said on the condition of anonymity.

When news organizations reported that Mr. McCain had written letters to government regulators on behalf of the lobbyist's client, the former campaign associates said, some aides feared for a time that attention would fall on her involvement.

Mr. McCain, 71, and the lobbyist, Vicki Iseman, 40, both say they never had a romantic relationship. But to his advisers, even the appearance of a close bond with a lobbyist whose clients often had business before the Senate committee Mr. McCain led threatened the story of redemption and rectitude that defined his political identity.[30]

The story never produced any real evidence of an affair, only the suspicions of two anonymous aides. Yet the article began with the suggestion of impropriety. Responding to a storm of criticism, *Times* ombudsman Clark Hoyt objected to the sexual emphasis of the article: "if you cannot provide readers with some independent evidence, I think it is wrong to report the suppositions or concerns of anonymous aides about whether the boss is getting into the wrong bed."[31]

Sometimes the use of suggestive verbs, like "may," "perhaps," "seems," and "appears," are more appropriate than more definitive words, like "is" or "will." The best an author can do at times is to say something "appears" to be the case, perhaps describing something that can't be observed, like a person's motive. But these words can also be used to convey a false impression. That happens when the evidence presented in the article falls short of establishing that what the author implies is likely to be true.

4. Lack of context: Civil rights leader Rev. Jesse Jackson once said that "text without context is pretext."[32] In July, 2010, the late conservative blogger Andrew Breitbart provided an example. He posted a video that appeared to show Shirley Sherrod, the Georgia rural development director for the U.S. Department of Agriculture, admitting discrimination against whites. The video, however, was maliciously doctored. The unedited version, which surfaced a few days later, showed just the opposite: how Mrs. Sherrod had *overcome* her bitter feelings about whites, who had murdered her father, to help a white farmer with a government aid program. But before the truth came out, Ms. Sherrod had been vilified by Fox News' Sean Hannity and Bill O'Reilly (the latter later apologized). She was fired from her job and denounced by the NAACP faster than a knee jerks when struck by a doctor's rubber mallet, only to be reinstated and praised days later by shame-faced officials.[33]

Taking comments out of context is hardly a tactic of conservatives alone. On Jan. 3, 2008, Republican presidential candidate John McCain interrupted a question at a campaign stop. It began, "President Bush has talked about our staying in Iraq for 50 years..." Mr. McCain cut in to say, "Maybe a hundred." Then he added, "We've been in Japan for 60 years. We've been in South Korea for 50 years or so. That'd be fine with me as long as Americans are not being injured or harmed or wounded or killed."[34]

Liberal and Democratic Web sites, political opponents, even some news programs such as "Democracy Now," reported the "hundred years" quip but not the important qualifier – "as long as Americans are not being injured." It made McCain appear insensitive to the human and monetary costs of the war.

At minimum, context requires us to consider the occasion or location of the words quoted. An offhand joke in an informal setting may reveal something about the source's character. But it would be interpreted quite differently as an official pronouncement. Thus, in 1984, when President Ronald Reagan spoke into a microphone he thought was off and quipped, "We begin bombing in five minutes," the meaning attached was quite different than had it been knowingly said in a public forum ... or to the Strategic Air Command.

It can still be difficult to detect a lack of context, but the Web now offers multiple versions of major stories, particularly at the national and international level. Try to find reports from news organizations operating across bias fault lines, such as nationality or political ideology. Check reports against each other to fill in missing or misleading emphases. Increasingly, online news articles are followed by comment boxes. Sometimes (amid considerable flatulence) you'll find context there. Pay particular attention to reactions from those sources named in the article. More on this in the final chapter.

5. Flawed comparisons: These comprise two general types — incomplete comparisons and apples to oranges.

Incomplete comparisons

If crime, disease, accidents, test scores, gasoline prices, inflation, or what-have-you is up or down, or if anything is better or worse, always ask, "compared to what?" At minimum, the comparison should include raw numbers and a percentage increase or decrease from a previous or baseline period, e.g., the average price of a gallon of regular gasoline in the U.S. rose 20 cents last month, a 5 percent increase from $4. Both numbers are needed because when the base is small, even a little change can represent a large percentage. Add one to one and you have only one more, but a 100% increase. At the other extreme, if the base is very large, even a substantial increase in number may represent only a small percentage change.

Comparisons also ought to include contextual baselines. Saying the average tuition charged by American universities has increased fourfold from 1980 may be misleading without a comparison to the overall inflation rate. Almost everything is more expensive now than it was 30 years ago. It would be more accurate to compare the increase in tuition in constant dollars, so it's not exaggerated by inflation. Or to compare the proportion of a typical family's income that's consumed by tuition then versus now.

If a trend is claimed there must be at least three data points, preferably more, over a reasonable period of time. That period should be long enough for whatever is being measured to change beyond the range of normal fluctuations. Weekly tallies of new claims for unemployment benefits, for example, bounce around enough that a clear picture of employment trends ought to stretch across at least a month, preferably six months to a year.

Inappropriate comparisons

Our understanding of anything new is shaped by the familiar, so comparisons abound in news and information. The Great Recession that began in 2007 was compared to the Great Depression. In the 1960s South Vietnam was conceived as a "falling domino" in the creation of a worldwide communist empire, rather than an anti-colonial nationalist movement that represented little threat to the United States.

Superficial similarities can mask differences so large the comparison is misleading. In 2002 Saddam Hussein was cast as the new Hitler. It made him seem more threatening and bolstered the case for war. While both were brutal dictators who gassed some of their countrymen, the scale and context of these atrocities and the power of the Iraqi vs. Nazi war machines relative to their neighbors was clearly a peanut to pumpkin comparison. As I write, another national leader, Israeli Prime Minister Benjamin Netanyahu, is invoking comparison with the Nazis, this time with Iraq's neighbor Iran. On March 28, 2012, *New York Times* former Jerusalem Bureau

Chief Ethan Bronner wrote: "For Mr. Netanyahu, an Iranian nuclear weapon would be the 21st century equivalent of the Nazi war machine and the Spanish Inquisition — the latest attempt to destroy the Jews."[35]   Before you accept a comparison, check for both qualitative and quantitative similarities.

6. Mistaking correlation for causation: Brain researchers have a saying about brain cells — neurons: "What fires together, wires together." The architecture of the brain is associational.[36] So it's not surprising that we often think that because two things happen at about the same time, one causes the other. In its eagerness to report diet and medical breakthroughs, the press may jump on studies that associate some risk or benefit with a particular vitamin, herb, diet, or exercise regime. Remember the fascination with vitamin C, beta-carotene, vitamin E, and eight glasses of water a day? None fulfilled early expectations. As I write, Vitamins E and D are being stripped of their capes and super powers, and coffee is in the telephone booth shedding its mild mannered reputation and emerging as a "wonder drug" protecting against prostate cancer, stroke, breast cancer, diabetes, liver disease and Parkinson's.[37]

Scientists require at least three conditions to be met before saying A likely caused B. First, A must precede B. Second, A and B must be correlated or associated in some predictable way. (For example, an increase of A, say proportion of people vaccinated, leads to a decrease of B, perhaps an illness.) Third, the relationship between A and B must not be a mere coincidence. An example is the association of ice cream sales and drownings. They may rise and fall together, but a third variable, the hot summer sun, explains the correlation. The heat both entices us into the water and makes us crave a frozen treat.

"That very issue of correlation and causation is key to anything you have to say about any kind of social science research."[38]

~ Edward Schumacher-Matos, National Public Radio ombudsman

Causality, like truth, is a human construct. Careful observation and logical inferences may build a body of evidence that A causes B, but because humans see reality incompletely and subjectively, we can never be absolutely sure there's no other factor really causing B. Science can never finally *prove* that A causes B, only that it's *probable*.

Complicating matters, the conditions that affect us most have *multiple* causes. An economic recession, for example, may be fathered by the combination of lax government regulation of financial markets, a wave of defaults on house mortgages, and a contraction of money to lend. Furthermore, *different sets of causes* can lead to the same effect. A recession might be caused primarily by the puncture of a speculative "bubble" in stock prices, or by excessive national debt, or by a sharp rise in the cost of oil and other basic commodities.

Nevertheless, the notion of cause and effect helps us reduce the great buzzing confusion of life to a more manageable set of patterns. These increase our ability to understand, predict, and sometimes control what's happening around us. Such utility makes claims of cause and effect common components of news and information.

Most leaps from correlation to causation involve more plausible links than between ice cream cone sales and drowning. An example is the idea that watching sexually explicit programs leads to fooling around. Consider how this front-page *Washington Post* story from 2008 begins:

Teenagers who watch a lot of television featuring flirting, necking, discussion of sex and sex scenes are much more likely than their peers to get pregnant or get a partner pregnant, according to the first study to directly link steamy programming to teen pregnancy.

The study, which tracked more than 700 12-to-17-year-olds for three years, found that those who viewed the most sexual content on TV were about twice as likely to be involved in a pregnancy as those who saw the least.

"Watching this kind of sexual content on television is a powerful factor in increasing the likelihood of a teen pregnancy," said lead researcher Anita Chandra. "We found a strong association." The study is being published today in Pediatrics, the journal of the American Academy of Pediatrics.[39]

"Watching ... is a powerful factor" equates *correlation* (those who watched the most sexual content were more likely to impregnate or become pregnant than those who watched the least) with *causation* (watching those shows was a *cause* of those teen pregnancies). It's possible that watching such programs is a cause of teens becoming sexually active, but this study does not, indeed cannot, prove that. By its design, it doesn't establish time order — that the TV watching preceded the sexual activity. What if sexually active teens prefer such programming more than abstinent ones who may find it distasteful? In other words, what if becoming sexually active leads to watching more adult programs?

7. The fundamental attribution error: In our individualistic American culture, we tend to over-emphasize personal *character* to explain other people's behavior and underestimate the surrounding *circumstances*. Social psychologists call this reasoning flaw the fundamental attribution error (FAE) because it's so prevalent, so commonsensical.[40]

Ironically, our desire to protect our self-esteem appears to override the FAE in one instance -- when *we* misbehave.[41] Then we're only too happy to blame circumstances and absolve our character. Thus the jerk down the street speeds because he disregards others' safety. It's his heedless character. But we speed when we're in a hurry. The circumstances warrant it. Harvard ethicist Michael J. Sandel provided a real world example: In Congressional hearings Wall Street bankers pointed to difficult circumstances beyond their control to explain the financial collapse of 2008. They were not responsible for the losses at their firms, they maintained. But a year earlier when the economy and their companies were doing well, *voila!* they *were* responsible — and thus deserved their lavish salaries.[42] We're good at looking for situational causes when our own behavior is called into question, but otherwise, we discount it.

Of course, character does count. Those who develop virtuous habits often make better decisions for themselves and others even under adverse circumstances. But the evidence for the situation *also* affecting our actions is overwhelming.[43] People who grow up in desperately poor, crime-ridden neighborhoods that lack successful role models (psychologists say, "you have to see it to be it") and effective schools, are much more likely to be arrested than those who grow up in safe neighborhoods with good schools, positive role models and financially secure parents.[44] Such spirit-sapping social conditions breed crime as surely as stagnant pools are nurseries for mosquitoes. Yet we routinely attribute people's success or failure almost entirely to character.

It's profitable to exploit the FAE

The FAE is a logic short circuit that news media exploit with saturated crime coverage. In addition to being cheap to gather, episodic reports of law-breaking — especially violent incidents such as murder, assault and rape — attract a large audience. Fresh cases occur daily. In both text and video, they've become a news staple, like grains at the bottom of the nutrition pyramid. But relatively few stories explore the social conditions and political decisions that encourage criminal behavior, much less the solutions to such problems.[45] The implication? It's personal. Some people simply choose to break the law. Circumstances are irrelevant, not worth reporting.

Talk shows on TV, and particularly radio, boil over with this unsophisticated way of presenting the world. Many hosts sow resentment to reap ratings. Sometimes big corporations or the wealthy are demonized. But more often these pundits assail liberal defenders of the poor, especially the black and brown poor, who are described as parasites extracting tax dollars from those who work hard and play by the rules.[46]

Social consequences

This simplistic way of thinking and reporting has serious consequences. Take the criminal justice system as a case in point. If you think crime is caused by people who are inherently bad, punishing them with lengthy jail terms seems appropriate. As a result, we Americans have the highest documented incarceration rate in the world.[47] California, which jails more of its residents than any other state, is currently on track to spend more on prisons than higher education within a few years.[48] And rather than focusing on rehabilitation that might assist inmates returning to society to become productive tax-payers, California punishes them in over-crowded conditions that render them angry and unfit for employment.[49] After serving time, punitive laws deprive felons of rights to vote, eligibility for public housing, food stamps and other forms of assistance. In seeking work they are usually asked to reveal any convictions, further crimping their chances for employment.[50] Seventy percent return to prison within a year — at considerable cost in terms of police and courts, not to mention the toll on victims of subsequent criminal behavior.[51] Assuming *people* are bad, rather than the *circumstances* of their upbringing, perpetuates the crime problem and creates a drag on the whole of society, not just the target population.

L: What is *Left out* or marginalized?

It's usually more difficult to notice what's missing or consigned to the margins than what's present and center stage. Consequently, omission and marginalization are among the most powerful and subtle means of introducing bias. They can be either intentional, subconscious or simply an oversight. The effect, however, is the same: an incomplete description of an event or issue renders a warped impression. The degree of distortion corresponds to the extent that what's missing is important to making sense of the news or information.

We are all practitioners of manipulation by omission and marginalization. Who among us volunteers our warts to potential employers or romantic interests? And when confronted, who doesn't downplay his/er flaws. Institutions — corporate and governmental — are no different in their relations with news media and the public.

In the spring of 2008, official Chinese news media focused on the violence of Tibetans protesting for greater freedom from China's government while eliminating from the picture any sign of violence on the part of Chinese police. Further, state media described Chinese investment in boosting the standard of living in Tibetan provinces but not suppression of Tibetan culture. It was a carefully managed, one-sided picture. And it was apparently effective across most of China in generating public sympathy for the government and resentment of Tibetans.[52]

Omission is most obvious when a controversy emerges and one side is quoted, but not the other. Or one side is allowed to speak both for themselves and for their opponent. Omission is least perceptible when a small piece of the mosaic of an issue or event is missing. For example, in the run-up to the Anglo-American invasion of Iraq, most Americans were ignorant of bitter disputes within government intelligence agencies over how the Bush administration was using the data about Iraq. "Many journalists knew about this, yet few chose to write about it," wrote Michael Massing in the *New York Review of Books*.[53] It was the failure to include legitimate dissenting voices within the U.S. intelligence community that led the *Times* to apologize for its pre-war reporting on May 26, 2004.

To find missing facts, look for missing stakeholders

Often missing facts are linked to missing stakeholders. The most likely to be overlooked are the least powerful. To see which individuals or groups affected by the matter at hand should be included, but aren't, try this: After reading the story, list the major stakeholders. Then go through the news or information a second time and note:

1. Which individuals or groups are included and which are not? Do those included have at least one person in a leadership role speaking for the group?

2. Which individuals or groups are mentioned most, particularly in the top half of the article (since readership drops off with length), and which least?

3. Which stakeholder's views are privileged and which are marginalized? Privileged viewpoints are ones that shape the direction of the article, perhaps becoming the angle or frame the reporter chooses for the premise of the story – usually the lead. Marginalized viewpoints are mentioned only in passing or challenged either by the author or another source.

Let me conclude with a humbling caution. The SMELL test can make it more difficult to fool you, but not impossible. A clever information-provider can selectively interview, selectively quote, selectively point the camera, and selectively edit to deceive us. If the topic is unfamiliar, we may strain to know what doesn't make sense and to recognize what has been left out. More than once during my doctoral dissertation when

I was able to accompany local television journalists in the field, I witnessed them grossly misrepresent reality in a way only those who were present would recognize. That's why detecting bias should be a *social* enterprise. How it can be will be addressed in the final chapter. But first we must add one more tool to our detective kit — how to "read" video and images.

7

Detecting Bias in Images

Behold these striking pictures. But as you behold them, beware of them, for they are not real. They are fake, the products of media consultants and spin-control artists who are trying to move you or deceive you or persuade you.

~ Kiku Adatto, author of *Picture Perfect*

Man 2.0, also known as Homo Sapiens, evolved some 200,000 years ago, anthropologists estimate. During the last quarter of that period — about 50,000 years ago — humans began to communicate with images. But written language appeared much more recently, just 5,000 to 6,000 years ago. And it began as glyphs, or picture writing — symbols that looked like what they were intended to represent.[1] We have evolved as visual animals. That's why images possess extraordinary persuasive power and can be remembered more easily than words.

Images — moving and still — have never played a greater role in news and information. Text was king in the era of books and newspapers. But videos, photos and data displays are usurping the throne as information moves from paper to pixels. This chapter explores four propositions to help us avoid being fooled by images:

1. Our brains process images in almost the *opposite* way that they make sense of words.

2. Image logic differs radically from text logic.

3. Images are easily manipulated.

4. We can learn to "read" images, though never as clearly as text.

In news and information, words and images usually complement each other. But as media ecologist Neil Postman and others have pointed out, they are entirely different ways of communicating. And their effects on us, even the way our brains process them, differ greatly.[2]

1. Our brains process images in almost the opposite way that they make sense of words

Words are abstract symbols, squiggles or sounds standing for something else. However, the images that appear most often in news and information — photos and videos — almost always directly represent something physical and real. You can't photograph an idea. Photos and videos are concrete and specific. They can't describe abstractions — concepts, theories, hypotheticals, and arguments. While words can generalize, photos and video clips are always anecdotal. They show a part, but not all, of what happened.

Words are consumed in linear fashion, printed left to right in most Western languages, on lines that proceed from top to bottom. It's like eating corn on the cob. Words require structure. To make sense, they must be arranged logically into sentences, paragraphs, and maybe chapters. When we read, the analytical left brain does the heavy lifting. However, images are consumed holistically, all at once like a grape. They don't require context, but convey meaning standing alone. The more intuitive right brain does the processing.

While we may know how to question whether the words of a text constitute a logical argument or truthful representation, we tend to just accept photos and videos as accurate depictions of reality. Typically, we don't apply logic to pictures. We simply react to their aesthetic quality or emotional punch.

A picture, we say, "is worth a thousand words." And "seeing is believing." We assume not only that they show what is real but, even more importantly, that they are *representative* of the event or issue in the news. Some news images seem to capture an event so powerfully that they are burned into our memories. It might be the airliner striking the second World Trade Center tower on Sept. 11, 2001. For Iraqis, perhaps the degrading photos of prisoners on leashes at the Abu Ghraib prison. For Afghanis, a video of Marines urinating on Taliban corpses. For baby boomers, it might be a naked Vietnamese girl burned by napalm running down a street shrieking in pain.[3] For Egyptians it might be video of police beating "the girl in the blue bra."

Photo from NPR on Tumblr

Images are powerful enough that governments work hard to suppress negative ones. In 2008 China blocked images of protesters in Tibet, and particularly the crackdown against them. Zimbabwe expelled foreign reporters who were recording attacks on members of the political opposition. Israel refused to let foreign journalists enter Gaza to cover its invasion at the end of 2008. Syria prohibited outside journalists from covering street demonstrations and a bloody crackdown on protestors that began in 2011. In the U.S. during World War II, military censors forbade publication of photos of dead American soldiers to avoid morale problems. In Viet Nam, on the other hand, photographers were free to cover the conflict. Televised images of the fighting — the "living room war" — were thought to have been a major cause of the nation's eventual disenchantment with the struggle.[4] Subsequently, the U.S. military resumed its restrictions. Between 1991 and 2009, photographers were barred from filming even the coffins of American soldiers flown home from Iraq.[5]

2. Image logic differs radically from text logic

The Canadian scholars Harold Innis and Marshall McLuhan believed that the medium was *as*, if not *more*, important than the message it conveyed.[6] Professor Postman advanced only a slightly less technologically-determined view of communication. In his delightful book, *Amusing Ourselves to Death*, he argued that the printed word enables ordered, logical, abstract reasoning — just what the public needs to solve complex problems in a democratic fashion. However, visual media — especially photography and videography — are too imprecise and emotionally-arousing for the conversation of democracy. They are more suited to entertain than inform.

As television supplanted print as America's dominant mass medium during the second half of the twentieth century, Dr. Postman predicted that we would come to prefer diversion to rational public decision-making. The proper use for a television, he advised, is to prop up one end of a book shelf or provide light for reading.

Television introduces two other differences between images and words. When photos are seen at 30 frames per second, the standard pace of video, they wash over us so quickly that they outpace our ability to critically assess them. We can slow down or re-read a section of text. We can stop and think. But a television broadcast is fleeting, always moving on. We can usually stop and replay a video on the Web, but TV has trained us to watch without interruption. It's also easier to maintain emotional distance in print. Video engages both our eyes and ears in a life-like presentation. We are much more likely to cry at a movie than while reading a book.

These characteristics make video the medium of choice for persuasion. Advertisers selling autos, skin creams, and political candidates value its emotional force and too-fast-for-analysis pace. Watching a screen also tends to be a more passive activity than reading. It may catch us with our skepticism shields down. Two University of Chicago researchers reported: "Television viewing was found to be a relatively unchallenging activity requiring little cognitive investment and consistently tied to feelings of relaxation, passivity, and drowsiness."[7]

Perhaps the most important difference between words and images is this: The meaning of images arises not from the proposition-then-evidence structure of words organized into sentences and paragraphs, but from mere association. In a photo or video, advertisers put happy, sexy, wealthy, or accomplished people together with a product to imply that the two are related, even that one causes the other. Were someone to put in words the message that drinking Coors Light or driving a BMW will make you hip and irresistible, you'd laugh. Put the same "statement" in a photo or video, however, and advertisers are willing to bet millions that we'll buy it.

3. Images are easily manipulated.

You might think that fauxtography began in 1989 when *TV Guide* magazine wanted to feature Oprah Winfrey on its cover, but had no photo showing the TV hostess after her successful diet. So they severed dancer Ann-Margaret's head from her curvaceous body and replaced it with Oprah's beaming countenance. "The truth is, however, that photography lost its innocence many years ago," noted Dartmouth College researcher Hany Farid.

Photo from legendsrevealed.com

"The nearly iconic portrait of the U.S. President Abraham Lincoln (circa 1860), for example, was a fake, and only the beginning of a long history of photographic trickery."[8]

Every year, altering images created with cameras becomes easier to accomplish with software such as Photoshop, and harder for consumers to detect. Fashion magazines alter photos routinely to gild Hollywood lilies. Even respected news media occasionally doctor images. *Time* magazine infamously darkened its cover photo of football legend and murder-suspect O.J. Simpson in 1994. The lesson? Seeing such images should never lead directly to believing. Consider the integrity of the source.

Digitally altering photos and videos is a relatively new and powerful technique. But it's far from the only way to manipulate the audience's reception of images. Subjects have long been posed to create a more dramatic impact. Even minor adjustments in camera placement or the angle of the lens can change our perception. A small demonstration can seem large in a close-up; a substantial group can seem small in a long shot or a panorama. A realtor with a fish-eye lens can make an apartment fit for a mouse look roomy enough for a moose. The camera's height relative to the subject also matters. People shot from above seem smaller and less powerful than those shot from a level plane. Those shot from below seem more powerful.

Consider this photo of Republican presidential hopeful Mitt Romney on the front page of the *New York Times* on January 18, 2012:

Photo from NewYorkTimes.com

Shot from above and at a distance, it conveyed a message that was reinforced by the caption that ran below it: "At a rally for Mitt Romney on Tuesday at the civic center in Florence S.C., the crowd seemed dwarfed by the setting." The Romney campaign certainly couldn't have been happy with the subtly negative impression that Romney could not draw a larger crowd in a conservative Southern state.

Possibly as a compensation call, the very next day in the same prominent place above the fold on the front page, the *Times* ran this photo, with the caption: "Leader and target: Mitt Romney drew a crowd in Spartanburg, S.C., but he also drew a barrage of attacks from rivals."

Photo from NewYorkTimes.com

Notice how greatly the camera angle and focal point differed from the previous day's rally photo. Many faces, rapt attention, the American flag centered in the frame — it appears to be an attempt by the *Times* to balance the previous day's most prominent image with a positively-charged photo. (Betcha my daughter's Barbie collection that Romney's aides raised hell with the editor for the previous day's photo!)

As the *Times*' photos demonstrate, focal point powerfully influences interpretation. People or events in the foreground always seem more important than those in the background. Even production values can make a difference, sometimes in surprising ways. Jumpy video shot from a handheld camera often conveys a greater sense of authenticity than video shot from a stable tripod. Cell phone images from bystanders at newsworthy events can generate as great a response as a professional photographer's. Circulated on the Internet, television, and newspapers, the amateur video of the beating of "the girl in the blue bra" generated rage and demonstrations around the world, even an explicit condemnation from U.S. Secretary of State Hillary Clinton.

Because of time and space limitations in most media — as well as the audience's attention limitations — one or a just a few photos or video clips represent an *entire* event whether or not they typify what happened. Because media images compress meaning into a few frames, they always introduce some level of distortion. They always show just one facet of the event despite the best efforts of photojournalists to honestly record what's taking place.

Intentional manipulation can occur through a series of choices. Commercial bias can be conveyed by choosing to cover a raucous street protest rather than more consequential, but visually static, "talking heads" inside a meeting room discussing new laws or policies. Or by going to where demonstrators are confronting police rather than where they are peacefully presenting their views in speeches. In addition to characterizing the entire protest by its most violent component, this has the effect of encouraging violence to gain publicity.

Political slant can arise from pointing the camera at a bleeding demonstrator but not a cop on a stretcher (or vice versa). Or focusing on an outrageous sign by placing it in the foreground while consigning the more reasonable ones to the blurred background.

These choices are usually made back in the newsroom, when editors pick the most dramatic photo from the 100 others the photographer took, or when they cut and paste together a composite minute of the most emotional video clips from an hour of recording.

Manipulating the media by controlling images

So far, we've examined distortions of reality introduced by whomever is operating the camera and selecting which images to exhibit. Now let's look at how those in *front* of the camera manipulate media images. Those with the resources and the authority to design the visual background — the "sets" — for news stories usually understand the power of images very well.

They are also familiar with the media's craving for compelling pictures.

"We absolutely thought of ourselves, when we got into the national campaign, as producers. We tried to create the most entertaining, visually attractive scene to fill that box, so that the cameras from the networks would have to use it."[9]

~ Michael Deaver, campaign manager for President Ronald Reagan

In a surprisingly candid interview with PBS host Bill Moyers, Michael Deaver argued that the visuals he orchestrated for network cameras made journalists unwitting instruments of President Reagan's political campaign. Mr. Deaver contended that the messages conveyed by these images overpowered any skeptical words reporters might employ to dim their impact. Words are as effective against images as rocks against tanks.

Karl Rove, President George W. Bush's political advisor, followed Mr. Deaver's playbook. He repeatedly staged presidential speeches with a background of preselected, friendly audiences, often ranks of military personnel. In May, 2003 President Bush could have announced the end of major combat operations in Iraq in May 2003 from the White House. Instead he donned a pilot's green flight suit and was flown across the continent to an aircraft carrier off the coast of San Diego bedecked with a giant "Mission Accomplished" banner. The dramatic flourish made the president look like a war hero. (Now, when so much video is archived on the Web, choreographed photos can boomerang. As the fighting continued, these same images were used against Mr. Bush.)

Still naive after all these years

Even though we live in the era of easy digital manipulation of images, we still react to pictures as if they convey reality. The doctored video Andrew Breitbart posted on the Web was naively taken as proof that Shirley Sherrod was a racist, not just by casual viewers, but by Agriculture Secretary Tom Vilsack who called her on her cell phone to fire her, and by, of all groups, the NAACP whose mission is to advance the cause of people of color. Both were wiping digital egg from their faces within days.

But less than a year later in the spring of 2011, officials in Washington had still not learned to be skeptical of video from partisan sources. That's when conservative activist James O'Keefe posted secretly recorded video of a luncheon between National Public Radio's chief fund-raiser Ron Schiller and two of O'Keefe's confederates posing as potential Muslim donors. The video appeared to show Mr. Schiller denigrating Republicans and members of the Tea Party. However an analysis of the original video, conducted by Pam Key of The Blaze, Glenn Beck's Web site, demonstrated that Mr. Schiller's comments and reactions had been manipulated to make his statements more offensive than they were in reality.[10] By that time, however, NPR's president had been fired and prominent Congressional Republicans had launched a campaign to end government support for NPR.

4. We can learn to "read" images, though never as clearly as text

With just a little effort, the visual bias detector on the next page can help to unravel both the choices and the logic of images to reveal underlying patterns. That's useful because most of the time we don't really notice how our attention is being steered.

Image Bias Detector				
Stakeholder Groups				
Group's name				
Foreground/ Background				
Active (aggressor?)/ Passive (victim?)				
Sympathetic /Neutral/ Un-sympathetic				
Primary Emotion Elicited				

A. Which stakeholders in the article are *not* included in the image(s)?
_____.

B. What is the "message" of the image(s)?
_____
_____.

C. Is this "message" consistent with the accompanying article? _____.
If not, how does it differ?
_____
_____.

D. Which biases, if any, are conveyed by the image(s)?
_____.

Here's how to use it:

Across row one, examine the article accompanying the image(s) and list the principal stakeholders. For each stakeholder group included in the image(s), note whether it is in the foreground — the part of the image that is clearest and usually in the "front" and center of the frame — or in the background.

Next examine whether members of each stakeholder group are portrayed as active (doing something to others or to the environment) or passive (having something done to them). If the image shows a conflict, note whether members are shown as aggressors or victims.

In row four, indicate whether the image represents each stakeholder group as worthy of our sympathy, our antipathy, or neither. In the final row, name the emotion each image arouses in you toward each group's members.

What's not included in a photo is as important as what is. In question A, the detector directs your attention at those stakeholder groups affected by the news, but left out of the image(s) accompanying the story. If a major group is ignored both in the story and the image(s), we should wonder whether the omission expresses bias against that group, perhaps that they "don't count."[11]

Question B asks for your impression of what the image "says." Consider what emotion it pulls from you and to whom it directs sympathy. Also keep in mind the meaning of camera placement and focal point.

In question C, you'll compare the main premise of the article to the message of the photo. In traditional news media, photos and text are gathered by different people. Editors generally select the photo that best illustrates the story. But if the image and story are contradictory, it may suggest a bias — that either the photographer or the author got it wrong. Question D asks you to put all of the information from the matrix and the preceding questions together. Is there a partisan bias in the image(s)?

Many news articles include one or more photos, drawings, or video clips. If there are more than one, you may need to analyze each with the detector. However, if they are similar, you may be able to group them together as if they were parts of one larger collage.

In print and the Web, a caption (or cutline) briefly describes or identifies an image and is usually placed under or next to it. Use it as an aide to interpreting the image, but focus mostly on the image itself.

Applying the matrix

Notice your reaction to the photo below, which ran on the front page of the *New York Times* on Aug. 10, 2008. It describes an incident in the brief war between Georgia and Russia. The caption reads: "A Georgian man wept over the body of a relative on Saturday after Russian airstrikes in Gori hit two apartment buildings." Two Georgian soldiers are also in the photo.

RUSSIA BROADENS MILITARY CAMPAIGN AS ALL-OUT WAR THREATENS GEORGIA

A Georgian man wept over the body of a relative on Saturday after Russian airstrikes in Gori hit two apartment buildings.

Photo from the New York Times

Do the photo and its accompanying caption move you with pity? For whom? Who look like the aggressors and who are the victims, according to this photo? Editors typically choose from scores or hundreds of photos those that support their news reports. In August, coverage in the *Times* emphasized Russian attacks and Georgian suffering. Editors chose photos like the one above. But three months later, the *Times* editors chose different photos taken at the same time as the first, as the story line began to reflect Georgian aggression in the contested South Ossetia region on the Russo-Georgian border.

Photo from NewYorkTimes.com

On Nov. 6, the *Times* ran the photo above with the caption: "Georgian forces fired rockets at South Ossetia in August." The headline read, "Georgia fired more cluster bombs than thought, killing civilians, report finds." One day later, a story headlined "Georgia claims on Russia war called into question" reported that "newly available accounts by independent military observers of the beginning of the war between Georgia and Russia this summer call into question the longstanding Georgian assertion that it was acting defensively against separatist and Russian aggression."[12]

In the first photo, the Russians are attacking and killing civilians. In the second, the Georgians may be doing the same.

Notice that in both cases the photographers were shooting from the Georgian side of the battlefield. As we discussed in chapter three, what you see depends on where you stand. During the conflict, the *Times'* coverage reflected a Georgian perspective and so did the first photo. Months later, when the other side of the story was told, *Times* editors chose an opposite photo. It's another reminder that even newspapers with standards as lofty as the *New York Times'* are writing the first draft of history. Real-time accounts of events, particularly large ones taking place over a geographic region, are always subject to revision.

If we ran the first photo above through the image bias detector, it would look like this:

Image Bias Detector			
Stakeholder Groups			
Group's name	Georgians	South Os-setians	Russians
Foreground/ Background	Fore-ground		
Active (aggressor?)/ Passive (victim?)	Passive/ victims		
Sympathetic /Neutral/ Un-sympathetic	Sympa-thetic		
Primary Emotion Elicited	Pity		

A. Which stakeholders in the article are *not* included in the image(s)? _South Ossetians,____Russians_____.

B. What is the "message" of the image(s)? _Pity the Georgian civilians killed by the Russian Air Force_____.

C. Is this "message" consistent with the accompanying article? Yes. If not, how does it differ?_____.

D. Which biases, if any, are conveyed by the image(s)? Pro-Georgian; anti-Russian._____.

Two Caveats

Researchers such as John Fiske have shown that television content is "read" differently by different audiences.[13] Because the "message" of images is not spelled out in words, viewers' interpretations will differ even more than in an analysis of text. These interpretations are likely to divide along the social fault lines described in chapter three. So collecting the impressions of a diverse group of evaluators will bolster the validity of any conclusion you might reach.

A second caution arises from the aforementioned tendency of media to rely on one or just a few visuals per story. No photo or video clip can tell the whole story of even a simple event, much less a complex issue. Nor can we reasonably expect all stakeholders to appear in the photos selected for publication. Therefore, *every* image reflects a bias, a subjective reduction of reality.

It's useful to note such bias. But be careful. The case for a partisan bias — as opposed to a bias for the common good — should be based on a *pattern of choices*. Take the photos of the 2012 Romney campaign shown above. Neither was doctored. Both were reflections of reality. But the first had a negative cast and the second positive for Mr. Romney. There was no *pattern* of bias. In contrast, most of the early photos of the

Russian-Georgian war reinforced a bias in the coverage that was pro-Georgian and anti-Russian. Only months later, in hindsight, did the *Times'* reporting and photo selection correct that early bias. To establish bias in images or video clips you have to ask: Of all possible images of any event, is there a pattern among those chosen that distorts reality?

Now that we've learned to detect bias in videos and photos, we're ready to consider how spinmeisters artfully combine words and images to climb inside our heads. We'll examine the most common tricks of the misinformation trade in the next chapter.

8

The Spinmeister's Art: Tricks of the Misinformation Trade

The customized manufacture of public discourse ... has become epidemic.

~ Stuart Ewen, author of *PR! A Social History of Spin*

At the dawn of the 21st century, America employs a record number of public relations agents — people with a talent for making a case to the public for the benefit of their clients. At the same time, we are laying off a record number of journalists — people skilled at breaking those cases open for the benefit of the public. In 1980 the ratio of public relations practitioners to journalists was nearly equal. By 2008, PR operatives outnumbered journalists by more than three to one.[1] *New York Times* media columnist David Carr described the result:

> There is a chance that historians will examine this period in American history and wonder if journalism left the field. In part, it is the triumph of the spinners, top to bottom. Since the media reached the height of its powers in the 1970s, there has been a pervasive effort to gain custody of public information in both the public and private sector. A working reporter cannot walk into a Gap store in a mall, let

alone a police station, and ask a question without being swarmed by bureaucracy.[2]

Lest you think Mr. Carr exaggerates, when his *Times* colleague David Barstow attended hearings on whom to blame for the massive Gulf of Mexico oil spill of 2010, he found "... there would be more PR people representing these big players than there were reporters, sometimes by a factor of two or three."[3]

This chapter explores three propositions:

1. **As professional journalism atrophies, public relations practitioners are growing bolder and more sophisticated.**

2. **We can predict when deception is most likely, thus know when to raise our level of skepticism.**

3. **The publicists' technique of choice is framing information to lead audiences in a particular direction without their noticing.**

Spinning facts to gain advantage or deflect responsibility is as old as Adam blaming Eve, who in turn blamed the serpent, for the consumption of forbidden fruit. But public relations as an occupation came into its own only in the 20th century. In 1900, news was carried on a single mass medium — the newspaper. In a scant hundred years, radio, then broadcast television, then TV on steroids with hundreds of cable and satellite channels, and finally the Internet have made media as common as air and its use as habitual as breathing. "The Media" overwhelmed older, often interpersonal, forms of telling news. Because news conveys the power to define the reality upon which people act, corporate and government officials began to deploy publicists to bend those media accounts to their own purposes. The White House did not name an official press secretary until Franklin Roosevelt became president in 1932.[4] Today even the First Lady has a press secretary and just about every corporation and government agency employs platoons of them. All because perception is power.[5]

"If you put a U.S. congressman in front of a microphone and ask what the weather is ... you're going to get spin. They're just constantly processing political consequences of every single word they utter."[6]

~ Bob Garfield, co-host of NPR's On the Media

1. As professional journalism atrophies, public relations practitioners are growing bolder and more sophisticated

Whether you loved it or loathed it, the administration of Dick Cheney and George W. Bush was unusually successful at manipulating a compliant news media during its first term. Every politician spins like a top, but the first administration of the new century spun on the scale of a planet. To spread its message, the government secretly paid journalists like Armstrong Williams, a commentator on education issues, to shill for its policies.[7] The government even created and distributed fake news with private contractors pretending to be reporters.[8]

Another ploy was to leak self-serving stories to the press and then cite the resulting coverage in interviews with other news media as "proof" of their validity. For example, Mr. Cheney's office told the *New York Times*, off the record, that U.S. intelligence agents had learned that Iraq had obtained thousands of high-strength aluminum tubes that could be used for enriching uranium to bomb strength.[9] The day the story was published, on Sept. 8, 2002, the vice president and National Security Advisor Condoleezza Rice appeared on Sunday morning network news talk shows.

Ms. Rice and Mr. Cheney explicitly cited the planted article, which ran on the front page of the *Times*, as evidence that Saddam Hussein was building nuclear weapons. On NBC's "Meet the Press," Mr. Cheney conveyed the impression that the information came *independently* from the prestigious newspaper: "There's a story in the *New York Times* this morning, and I want to attribute it to the *Times*."[10]

During the long and bitter war with those who opposed the Anglo-American occupation of Iraq, the administration developed a brilliant, if exploitive, strategy — to provide private Pentagon briefings and contracting business opportunities to retired military officers who acted as expert sources for mainstream news media. They enjoyed these benefits so long as they parroted administration talking points in their role as purportedly neutral military analysts. As the *New York Times* reported in 2008, "the Bush administration has used its control over access and information in an effort to transform the analysts into a kind of media Trojan horse — an instrument intended to shape terrorism coverage from inside the major TV and radio networks."[11]

"The muscles of journalism are weakening and the muscles of public relations are bulking up – as if they were on steroids."[12]

~ David Barstow, *New York Times* investigative reporter

A more recent highlight tape of political deception would include Sarah Palin's media-enhanced claim that the Obama Administration's health care reform included "death panels" deciding the fate of Medicare recipients. PolitiFact.com called "death panels" the "Lie of the Year" and FactCheck.org referred to it as one of their "whoppers" of 2009.[13] On the Web, political activists spread lies that President Obama was secretly a Muslim and born outside of the United States. In 2010, Andrew Breitbart posted the doctored video of Shirley

Sherrod mentioned in chapter six. And in March 2011, James O'Keefe posted his selectively edited sting of NPR.

Conservatives don't own spin. *Washington Post* fact-checker Glenn Kessler criticized Congressional Democrats for repeatedly mis-characterizing budget cuts they were offering Congressional Republicans during the debt ceiling debate of mid-2011.[14] And PolitiFact "awarded" Democrats the 2011 "Lie of the Year" for saying Republican Congressman Paul Ryan's plans for Medicare would kill the program. As Fact-check.org at the University of Pennsylvania has documented, both Democrats and Republicans have been guilty of distorting the factual record and smearing the other in campaign advertising and PR efforts.

Political and governmental spin may get the most attention, but for sheer volume, the prize for making the public dizzy goes to special interests outside of government. In her 2010 book, *Merchants of Death*, University of California - San Diego historian of science Naomi Oreskes addressed the growing gap between the scientific community's near-certainty and the public's rising doubt that human activity is warming the planet. In an NPR interview, she explained:

> There has been a systematic effort organized by people outside the scientific community to undermine the scientific data and to convince all of us that the scientific jury is still out in order to delay government, business and community action on taking steps to prevent further man-made climate change.[15]

A similarly self-serving effort at muddying public opinion about the health risks of smoking was executed by the tobacco industry during the last half of the 20th century.[16] Polluting the infosphere pays.

2. We can predict when deception is most likely, thus know when to raise our level of skepticism

See if this rings true:

$$\text{The probability of deception} = \frac{\text{The benefit to be gained or loss avoided}}{[\text{The cost of being exposed}] \times [\text{The likelihood of being exposed}]}$$

This occurred to me on a fine autumn afternoon during a two-hand-touch football game when the miscreant I was supposed to cover caught a pass and scampered for a touchdown. I dove at the artful dodger, but only one hand made contact with the tail of his t-shirt. To cover my shame, I claimed to have tagged him with two. Had a teammate caught him short of a touchdown, I would have copped to missing him. But the touchdown raised the value of the loss my deception avoided. Even though my credibility was on the line, I knew my lie could not be convincingly refuted. The Palo Alto Saturday Football and Ice Cream Society lacked instant replay capability. (Sigh ... and my mom used to call me "honest John"!)

Of course the costs and benefits of deception are calculated by the deceiver. We would have to infer their values — high, moderate or low — because we can't read their minds. But our estimates are likely to be useful in deciding when to take a fact-claim with a grain — or sack — of salt.

We should be most wary of fact claims when deception offers great benefit or avoidance of significant loss to the deceiver and there is either little cost to the deceiver if caught or only a slight chance that the misinformation will be exposed in time to negate the benefit. Before the First Gulf War, for example, the U.S. military led the press to believe that Kuwait would be invaded by sea.[17] The actual attack came through the desert. The benefit of misleading the press — and through them, the Iraqis — was for the Allies an almost casualty-free victory over Saddam Hussein's occupation forces. When the deception became obvious after the invasion, there was little cost. In war, it's almost assumed that the press will be used to gain strategic advantage. As Aeschylus noted 2500 years ago, "In war, truth is the first casualty." It's as true today during the "war on terror."

Knowing the track record of the information-provider also helps. During the Vietnam conflict, American reporters became so used to inflated accounts of the harm inflicted on the enemy, they called the military's evening briefings "the five o'clock follies."[18]

The likelihood that a deception will be discovered varies with the number of people who are aware of it, their personal stake in it, and the power of the deceiver to identify and punish anyone who would expose it. The fewer who know of the falsehood and the greater their stake in it, the less possibility one of them will disclose it intentionally or by accident. The Ponzi maestro Bernie Madoff, for example, shared the truth about his swindle with just a few associates who had as much to lose as he did were it to be revealed. The most secure conspiracies are small and the conspirators are like-minded. Additionally, the more certain it is that a whistleblower will be punished and the more severe the sanction, the less likely that it will be disclosed.

These conditions for successful deception are met most completely at the command levels of military and paramilitary forces, such as the CIA, FBI and police forces. Their employees are trained to obey leaders unquestioningly. They can face severe penalties for disclosing government secrets. Even being suspected of disclosure can bring punishment.[19] Although all of these agencies are branches of government, public access laws, such as the Freedom of Information Act, rarely succeed in forcing disclosure in time to head off adverse consequences. Finally, their opponents — nations or groups at war with us and those suspected of treason or crime — are unlikely to be considered credible disclosers should they be allowed to give their side of the story.

When leaders of such hierarchical government agencies speak, we are most vulnerable to being misled. When Secretary of Defense Robert McNamara assured Americans in the mid-1960s that the U.S. was winning in Viet Nam and when CIA Chief George Tenet confirmed White House claims of weapons of mass destruction in Iraq almost four decades later, we didn't learn that neither was true until hundreds of thousands of deaths later. The poet John Milton may have been correct when he famously wrote "Let [Truth] and Falsehood grapple; who ever knew Truth put to the worse in a free and open encounter?" But as Mark Twain observed, "A lie can travel halfway around the world while truth is putting on its shoes."[20] Falsehood can inflict irreversible damage before truth prevails.

Corporations cannot imprison those who would disclose deception, but they can fire them and jeopardize their careers by stigmatizing them as disloyal employees — not "team players." Corporations may also acquire the right to sue whistleblowers who have signed away their free speech rights in order to gain employment or separation benefits. Additionally, corporations operate beyond the reach of "sunshine" laws that open government meetings and documents to public inspection. Unlike legislative bodies elected by voters, candidates for corporate boards of directors are hand-picked by executives to ensure ideological consonance. Consequently, it is difficult to uncover corporate deception. The collapse of Enron in 2001 and the implosion of huge Wall Street investment firms that plunged much of the world into recession in 2007 were not foreseen even by the elite business press. To the contrary, *Fortune* Magazine named Enron as "America's Most Innovative Company" for six straight years prior to its bankruptcy.[21]

3. The publicists' technique of choice is framing information to lead audiences in a particular direction without their noticing

Outright lies are more likely to be exposed than half truths. And once exposed, they can lead mainstream journalists to become more skeptical of the source. So skillful PR agents operate in the twilight zone between truth and falsehood. Eric Alterman, a columnist at *The Nation*, described it this way: "They are able to provide data that for journalistic purposes is entirely credible. The information is true enough. It is slanted. It is propagandistic. But it is not false."[22] Recall again the story of Adam and Eve. The serpent offered an alluring half-truth to tempt Eve: humans would become like God in knowing good from evil. True enough, but he omitted the parts about multiplying the pain of childbirth, and a life of toil and sweat culminating in death.

The most common and successful means of influencing news coverage is through framing messages so they reflect well — or at least better than they might otherwise — on the agent's client. Framing covers a collection of techniques that subtly lead the audience in a particular direction. Frames lay down tracks for the audience's train of thought. They are effective to the extent that they trigger or activate a set of understandings in our heads about how the world works, or ought to work. They exert their greatest influence when we are least aware of them.[23]

What's common to all frames is that they exclude significant parts of the story, much as a picture frame encloses one part of a wider panorama and leaves everything else out. Because our senses engage with what's in the frame — including whatever prior knowledge it triggers in our brains — it's hard to notice what's *not* there. Frames grease the skids for consonant ideas and marginalize those outside their boundaries.

After Al Qaeda was revealed as the perpetrator of the murderous attacks of 9/11/2001, some liberals, such as University of California cognitive scientist George Lakoff, argued for a criminal justice frame: Find those responsible for the crime and bring them to justice. The administration of George W. Bush, however, chose a much broader frame – a "war on terror." Instead of an effort limited to finding and punishing Osama bin Laden and others associated with the 9/11 attack, the U.S. began what was to become America's longest war committing tens of thousands of U.S. soldiers and hundreds of billions of U.S. dollars to a war with an indigenous Afghan Islamist group calling themselves the Taliban ("students" in Arabic).

Once the "war on terror" frame was adopted, it appeared to make sense to support one side in an Afghan civil war (the Northern Alliance), to install a government and attempt to impose democracy by force on a tribal society deeply suspicious of outsiders and non-Muslims. The pursuit of Bin Laden, which would have been front and center in a criminal justice frame, became a secondary concern. It became almost irrelevant when the "war on terror" frame was used as justification for the subsequent invasion of Iraq. Regardless of which frame you think was most appropriate, the consequences of choosing one over the other brought the nation more than a decade of war and incurred more than a trillion dollars of national debt.

Inserting frames into text and images can be subconscious, due to the blinders of our national culture, class, race, gender, etc. Or it can be carefully crafted — propaganda. When it is intentional and serves a partisan interest rather than the common good, the polite term for it is "spin." For example, when Massey Energy's Upper Big Branch mine exploded on an April afternoon in 2010 killing 29 workers, the company framed the worst coal mining disaster in 40 years as "an act of god," a natural occurrence in an inherently dangerous occupation. After months of investigation, however, the federal government decided that failure to prevent the tragedy was an act of Massey and cited massive and routine neglect of safety procedures.[24]

Sources that journalists quote can be expected to spin, but the task of journalism is to expose such manipulation. And, of course, journalists should avoid spinning themselves.

> "I've often joked that if I ever write an autobiography, I'm going to title it, 'Waiting for people to lie to me.'"[25]
>
> ~ Veteran *Washington Post* reporter Glenn Kessler

The best journalists expose spin by challenging or contradicting it. They can either find a source to voice the challenge, or make their own statements, usually by way of adding context. If, for example, a source framed violence against a woman by saying "the way she dressed invited sexual assault," the journalist could quote an expert, who might say "violence against women is never justified by their appearance." Or add context, such as "Domestic violence laws in the state do not take the victim's appearance into consideration." But as journalism lapses into harried "churnalism," the task of noticing frames and avoiding the trap they spring on our thinking falls more and more to us as critical consumers.

Priming

A common framing device is priming. Polling prior to the March 2000 primary election in California demonstrated its power. Pollsters read accounts of a political ballot initiative to likely voters. In certain counties, a short summary of the proposition was read: "Proposition 21 provides changes for juvenile felonies – increasing penalties, changing trial procedures and required reporting." In those counties, likely voters said they opposed Prop. 21 by a 17-percentage-point margin over those who approved. But in other, similar counties, when pollsters added the following sentence — "The Juvenile Crime Initiative increases punishment for gang-related felonies, home invasion robbery, car-jacking and drive-by shootings, and creates a crime of gang-recruitment activities" — likely voters favored it by a 23-point margin. A one-sentence expansion of wording contributed to a 40-point difference in public opinion.[26] That's because phrases like "car-jacking," "gang," and "drive-by-shootings" conjure images in our mind's eye. These prime us to respond in a certain way by provoking emotions that we may act on without even noticing. Our brains are organized to automatically bring to mind associated memory traces.[27] Although the pollsters intended no manipulation, pundits and political and commercial message-makers frequently do.

Framing with value-laden words and phrases

One of the most common framing devices consists of choosing a *particular word or phrase* that is subtly loaded. Linguists have shown that words and phrases carry baggage, or "entailments." Professor Lakoff begins his framing classes at U.C. Berkeley by telling students: "Don't think of an elephant!" as an example of how impossible it is to encounter the word "elephant" and not think of one.

Examples of value-laden words and phrases in public discourse are as common as teeth in sharks. Take the word "progressive." That's what many political liberals now like to call themselves. It suggests that they favor progress. And it erroneously implies that non-progressives do not. Or the phrase, "free market." Almost every market is regulated — and therefore to some degree un-free. (Even the black market is regulated — by gangsters.) But those who favor market solutions have succeeded in joining the two words at the hip, giving the term a positive twist. Calling a tax cut, "tax relief," similarly implies something positive, a cessation of suffering or perhaps injustice. It suggests that taxes, which are necessary for any society to provide protection and build infrastructure, are inherently oppressive. Calling the federal inheritance tax a "death tax," makes it seem absurd and applicable to everyone who passes away rather than to the heirs of a tiny percentage of the population.

Another type of loaded term is the code word. It is designed to spark particular interpretations — usually negative — among some listeners without alarming others. During ABC's "This Week" talk show on Aug. 3, 2008, political commentator David Gergen accused Sen. McCain's campaign of coded racism against then-Sen. Obama:

> There has been a very intentional effort to paint him [Obama] as somebody outside the mainstream, other, 'he's not one of us.' I think the McCain campaign has been scrupulous about not directly saying it, but it's the subtext of this campaign. Everybody knows that. There are certain kinds of signals. As a native of the south, I can tell you, when you see this Charlton Heston ad, 'The One,' that's code for, 'he's uppity, he ought to stay in his place.' Everybody gets that who is from a southern background. We all understand that. When McCain comes out and starts talking about affirmative action, 'I'm against quotas,' we get what that's about.[28]

Framing by naming

In the book of Genesis, Adam gets to name all the animals of the earth. This symbolizes dominion over them. The same happens in news. Every partisan group tries to get the media to use its labels. Naming something can steer public interpretation and thus advance the namer's cause. Unless the name meets early and strong opposition, it's likely to be accepted, along with its ideological structuring of the situation.

For example, the administration of George W. Bush named its plan for a military attack on Iraq "Operation Iraqi Freedom." From that perspective the actions of U.S. and British military forces in March and April of 2003 could be called "liberation." That term elicits a more favorable response than a more neutral word like "invasion." Likewise, labeling Iraqis fighting U.S. forces as "terrorists" rather than "resistance fighters" stacks the deck in favor of the Americans. Some people may associate the term "resistance" with the French underground and others who heroically fought Nazi occupation.[29]

Similarly, calling the people under arms on one side "militants," "extremists," or "gunmen," and those on the other "the army," "police," or "soldiers" delegitimizes the first group in favor of the second. After all, isn't almost everyone in the police or army a "gunman" (or gunwoman)? And who is more militant than the military? Across the sweep of time, have soldiers always held the high moral ground versus less organized fighters? How about our own history? Were the Minutemen who fired on British Redcoats from behind trees less justified than their uniformed opponents?

Framing with stereotypes

Stereotypes are often used to frame people, places, and events. A stereotype is a generalization about all members of a group based on the characteristics of a few. They can be positive (Asians are good at math) or negative (men are insensitive and combative).

Stereotypes can be subtle. Have you noticed a tendency in the press to call well-spoken black people "articulate" but rarely apply the same term to white people? Under the surface, might the author be indicating surprise to find articulate African-Americans? And an assumption that most black people are inarticulate?

Similarly, the physical attributes of women may be commented upon much more often than those of men. Women may be called "matronly," for example. But we have no similar word for men. (Patronly?) The implied stereotype is that a woman's value lies in her appearance. Candidate Hillary Clinton's cleavage and ankles drew comment in political reporting in 2008, as did Florida Republican Katherine Harris' use of makeup back in 2004. What have these to do with their ability as political or government leaders?

Framing with themes

A fifth framing device is a *theme* running through a story. Consider how reporters at the *San Jose Mercury News* framed the death of a man who had fractured his wife's skull before dying in a hail of police bullets when he pulled a gun on officers investigating the beating:

> This is the story of Dan McGovern, who friends and family say loved cars, cops, guns and most of all, the woman he met after paying $3,000 to a professional matchmaking service.[30]

The article barely mentioned domestic violence. Instead it described a simple but good man, driven to apparent "blue suicide" by his consuming love for a manipulative foreign bride who had done him wrong. A female colleague of the reporters who wrote the story complained: "It's not a love story when a man beats a woman so seriously that she goes to the hospital with severe head injuries." Recognizing the bias, the *Mercury News* ran an article the following day that quoted several domestic violence experts contradicting the victim blame frame. [31]

Framing with metaphor and simile

Similes and metaphors constitute especially powerful framing devices. Both compare different things whose similarities help convey a point. What makes them so potent is the ability to transform something complex and perhaps not well understood into something simple and familiar that suggests a commonsense interpretation.

Metaphors and similes are wonderful instructional and story-telling tools, and thus they are of great value to journalists, particularly opinion writers. The danger is that we may overlook considerable differences in reality between the two things that are compared and be captivated by eloquence rather than convinced by evidence.

Major public policy debates are a good place to find these framing devices. Before the 2003 invasion of Iraq, Secretary of State Colin Powell used a simile for Iraq that came to be called the Pottery Barn rule: "If you break it, you own it."[32] At the time, Mr. Powell was cautioning the administration to think twice about going to war because it would incur a moral obligation to repair the damage to Iraq.

Notice the simplicity of the Pottery Barn rule – only seven words. And its familiarity. Who hasn't seen a sign like that in a store? Furthermore, the audience can see some similarity between the things being compared, as with all successful similes. A shattered country seems at least a little like broken pottery. Finally, the moral obligation in either case to offer restitution for the damage fits our cultural values so well we take it as common sense.

But what metaphors and similes *obscure* is as important as what they reveal. For starters, the Pottery Barn is made whole, indeed happy, by the purchase of the broken pot. But the dead in a war cannot be brought back. No restitution can compensate the thousands of Americans who lost their lives or limbs or the many-times-larger number of Iraqis killed or injured.

Further, unlike pottery, a nation is not up for sale. And the simile distracts us from a more central moral question: whether a nation may violate the United Nations charter to invade another country without first having been attacked. Breaking pottery doesn't violate international law; unprovoked invasion does.

Good journalists help the audience see through ideologically-loaded similes and metaphors employed by sources, and avoid creating them. But as journalism shrivels, the task falls to us. Whenever you hear a persuasive simile or metaphor, consider all the ways the two situations *differ*.

In the final chapter we turn to the growing number of ways the Internet allows us to break frames open to check the validity of news and information.

9

Online Tools for Sniffing Out Bias, Including Our Own

Know thyself.

~ Ancient Greek proverb

By this point I hope that bias in news and information has become more visible. But sometimes slant can be so subtle that we need help to detect it. Fortunately, the World Wide Web makes it possible, and sometimes easy, to accomplish this.

This chapter will explore five propositions:

1. We can — and ought to — become aware of our own biases (even though it may be as appealing as a colonoscopy).

2. Professional fact-checking organizations are popping up like mushrooms after a spring rain.

3. The Internet puts a virtual reference library at our fingertips 24/7, enabling us to conduct our own fact-checks.

4. Social media allow us to collaborate in vetting content with others who may be more knowledgeable.

5. The Web can even help us discover people and perspectives that are ignored or marginalized in mainstream U.S. media.

Socrates, the fifth century BCE father of western philosophy (and first suicide philosopher), left no writings, but his words deeply impressed his student Plato who quotes him saying, "The unexamined life is not worth living."[1] It's worth noting, however, that when Socrates examined the lives of jaded Athenians, they decided *his* was not worth continuing. As you may recall, they insisted he drink a fatal draught of hemlock. Examining our biases may not kill us, but it's likely to entail discomfort. As with a colonoscopy, it's not just the pain of ascending the down staircase; we're also afraid of what we might discover about ourselves.

1. We can — and ought to — become aware of our own biases

Our partisan biases distort how we perceive the world around us. When shared, they can create a culture of injustice, allowing us to rationalize discrimination and repression. Across history and in too many places today, prejudices based on religion, race, ethnicity, gender and sexual orientation have led to oppression, war, slavery, murderous pogroms and genocide. Unscrupulous leaders almost always play on popular biases and couple it with fear to catapult themselves to power. Our unexamined biases make us their pawns. Partisan biases divide 21st century American society, preventing us from seeing and embracing our common humanity, breeding indifference to others' suffering, resentment, even hatred.

Obstacles to introspection

While we may agree that we ought to identify our partisan biases, doing so is difficult for at least three interlocking reasons:

1. Cultural blindness — biases we share with those around us are difficult to notice because they seem normal or natural rather than distortions of reality.

2. Motivated blindness — our biases often buttress our selfish interests, sometimes even our self-esteem. Thus acknowledging them can create uncomfortable cognitive dissonance between what we have done or want to do and what we ought to do. If nothing else, it's painful to admit we're wrong. More painful still to accept guilt for actions the bias justified.

3. Social pressure — failure to share the biases of colleagues, friends and family can alienate us from them.

Have you ever been amazed that a nation of people as intelligent, educated, civilized, as *Christian*, as Germany's population was before World War II could have systematically executed six million fellow citizens simply because they were Jewish. Or wondered how slave owners in the ante-bellum South could have thought buying, selling and enslaving other humans was moral. Or that some families in Asia and the Middle East still consider the murder of their daughters "honor killings" because they were seen with a man from the "wrong" religion or caste.

Because of the fundamental attribution error (overestimating the influence of personal character on behavior and underestimating social circumstances), we tend to think of these people as moral reprobates, perhaps even monsters. We may like to think we would never act as they did, that our character is superior. But most of these people were average humans going along to get along with the biases of their culture and time. That doesn't exonerate them, but it does emphasize the importance of recognizing how bias undermines our sense of humanity.

Cultural blindness

Consider the case of the American South before the Civil War — and a century after it when you include the legal chains of Jim Crow legislation. If you happened to be born white, you grew up in a society where slavery, and later subjugation of blacks, was accepted as normal, even natural. It was based on the notion among whites that black people were childish, lazy, and mentally inferior. From that perspective, blacks needed the supervision of whites for their own good.

These racialist ideas were not confined to the Southern states. In 1859 the Supreme Court of the United States held that blacks were simply the property of their owners with no independent human rights. For centuries, following the voyages of Columbus, the notion of white superiority encouraged, and was used to justify, European colonization of other peoples around the globe.

Motivated blindness

Racial bias provided a ready rationalization for economic exploitation. In a cotton-farming economy dependent on slave labor, Southern plantation owners profited from "the peculiar institution." The money generated from the cotton trade also supported churches, local merchants and artisans. Arguments against slavery threatened the system that put bread on their tables. Even poor whites, though sometimes disdained as "trash" by wealthier classes and disadvantaged by competition from unpaid labor, received a boost to their self-esteem; they could console themselves with being "better" than blacks.

Imagine the anguish of even *considering* the humanity of black people: the brutality of slavery directly contradicted the fundamental demand of the dominant religion of the South — to love others as one's self. Those troubled by the cruelty of slavery, as was Thomas Jefferson, experienced a painful clash between their moral beliefs and actions. He wrote of slavery, "I tremble for my country when I consider that God is just." But he didn't liberate his slaves, nor refrain from taking sexual liberties with a slave woman.[2] Like other slave-holders, his racial bias supported his selfish interest. Even for this most brilliant and morally sensitive man, self-interest defeated conscience.

Social pressure

Failure to share racial bias, or to oppose it, led to dire consequences. Blacks who resisted slavery were beaten or killed. Their assailants faced neither legal consequences nor social disapproval. Quite the opposite, as photos and descriptions of lynchings demonstrate. Abraham Lincoln declared an end to slavery in the deep South in 1863, but for decades afterwards vigilantes such as the Ku Klux Kan terrorized blacks who would assert equal rights. The few whites who stood up for blacks were humiliated and ostracized as "nigger lovers." As historian Joel Williamson wrote: "White people could not prescribe and enforce a precise role upon black people without prescribing and enforcing a precise role upon themselves."[3] As late as the 1960s, blacks and whites who traveled to the South to promote the equal rights of African-Americans were jailed, beaten and sometimes killed.[4]

For blacks — and whites as well — racial bias was a heavily fortified, deeply entrenched prison that degraded both the inmates and the jailors. The Civil War that first breached that prison cost a greater number of American lives — the vast majority of them young *white* men — than World War I, World War II, Korea and Viet Nam combined.[5]

Racial bias, of course, was never confined to the South. Mob lynchings occurred as far north as Duluth, Minnesota (in 1920) and some of the worst rampages targeting blacks occurred outside the former Confederate States. While racism is no longer as virulent and discrimination is now prohibited by law, subtle bias against blacks remains as American as apple pie.[6]

Biases play an enormous role in American politics. Campaign ads fasten on prejudices like ticks on deer, generating fear and loathing of immigrants, homosexuals, religious minorities, the poor, people of color, unions, big government, and big corporations. Unfortunately, playing to such biases appears to work. "When it comes to political views, actual logic does not really change many people's views at least in the short term," argued James Fallows, national correspondent for *The Atlantic.* "If you look at the way political elections are carried out, and the way people make up their minds on large issues, it's partly logic, but it's also what you could think of as tribalism. It's loyalties to what the people you like think."[7]

How to uncover your biases

Surfacing your biases is a bit like the "examination of conscience" that Catholics are urged to undertake before confession. It demands ruthless honesty. Fortunately there are tools to help. Visit www.implicit.harvard.edu. There you can evaluate some of your own biases.

Project Implicit is based on the idea that we are often biased without knowing it, or at least without being willing to admit it. It has a bank of diagnostic quizzes you can give yourself to reveal deep predispositions for or against people based on race, disability, religion, sexual preference, size, etc.

The Implicit Association Test asks you to make snap associations between sets of positive and negative words and photos of people with different characteristics, such as skin color, ethnicity, or weight. For example, if you take longer to associate positive words with blacks than with whites and less time to connect negative words with blacks than whites, the researchers believe you may have a bias. Journalist Sally Lehrman wrote of Project Implicit:

> The team has studied automatic reactions through more than 5 million Web-based tests so far. About 80% of users have shown a preference for young over old. Nearly the same proportion of self-identified white people and

Asians have a more favorable impression of white faces relative to black ones. Users also prefer able-bodied people over those with limited physical abilities, straight people over gay and thin people over heavy ones.

Even more disturbing was that these biases operated below the level of conscious thought.

Our automatic reactions often don't match the conscious attitudes we hold, the researchers have found, and yet we act on them every day. Even though a majority of people explicitly expressed the opposite view, for instance, most test takers implicitly considered Native Americans less "American" than white citizens. Native Americans themselves, however, strongly disagreed. Asian Americans also fell short of belonging, according to users — even those who were Asian American themselves. The team discovered it was easiest for test-takers to associate harmless objects with white people. And what about black people? With them, users of all races found it easier to associate weapons.[8]

See how you do on these common prejudices: skin tone, religion, gender, race (blacks and whites), Asians, Arabs, age, disability, sexual preference, and weight. Make a note of the results. Consider that they might just indicate a set of biases that you carry. (Yes, I was embarrassed too! But don't feel bad. Making them visible is the first step toward easing their grip.)

2. Professional fact-checking organizations are popping up like mushrooms after a spring rain

Have you ever received a chain email that makes a startling claim about politics? Here's one a friend sent me in 2010 with the subject line: "A memory from 1987 (This is bone chilling!!!)." The text read:

It was 1987! At a lecture the other day they were playing an old news video of Lt. Col. Oliver North testifying at the Iran-Contra hearings during the Reagan Administration. There was Ollie in front of God and country getting the third degree, but what he said was stunning!

He was being drilled by a senator, 'Did you not recently spend close to $60,000 for a home security system?' Ollie replied, 'Yes, I did, sir.'

The senator continued, trying to get a laugh out of the audience, 'Isn't that just a little excessive?'

'No, sir,' continued Ollie.

'No? And why not?' the senator asked.

'Because the lives of my family and I were threatened, sir.'
'Threatened? By whom?' the senator questioned. 'By a Muslim terrorist, sir' Ollie answered.
'Terrorist? What terrorist could possibly scare you that much?'

'His name is Osama bin Laden, sir' Ollie replied.

Why are you so afraid of this man?' the senator asked.

'Because, sir, he is the most evil person alive that I know of,' Ollie answered, 'and the Muslims are trying to take over

America and destroy it from the inside out and putting their people into our political offices.'

'And what do you recommend we do about him?' asked the senator.

'Well, sir, if it was up to me, I would recommend that an assassin team be formed to eliminate him and his men from the face of the earth.'

The senator disagreed with this approach, and that was all that was shown of the clip. By the way, that senator was Al Gore!

My first reaction was "Poor Ollie, how dare Al Gore ridicule this clairvoyant!" Then I remembered something Columbia University journalism professor Sreenath Sreenivasan wrote about chain emails: though they may gain credibility from having been sent from a friend, consider the bias of the friend.[9]

My forwarding friend, whose Republican loyalties run as deep as orange in carrots, has strong libertarian views. I also noticed that there was no disclosure of who produced the email in the first place, a red flag as ominous as the Jolly Roger. So I typed the email's subject line into a Google search. Midway down the first results page was an entry from a Web site called **Snopes.com** (www.snopes.com) that debunks urban legends and other myths. It looked like this:

Snopes investigators consulted Lt. Col. North's testimony at the Iran-Contra Hearings in 1987 and found that he never mentioned Osama Bin Laden. Neither was he questioned by Sen. Gore. Snopes also reprinted a response from Lt. Col. North himself to the viral email. It read in part: "It was Committee Counsel John Nields, not a senator, who was doing the questioning. The security system ... cost $16K, not $60K. The terrorist who threatened to kill me ... was not Usama Bin Laden, it was Abu Nidal (who works for the Libyans — not the Taliban and not in Afghanistan)." Lt. Col. North began his disavowal this way: "Though I would like to claim the gift of prophecy, I don't have it."[10]

Determining the truth of this chain email would have been difficult and time-consuming for me, but fortunately there are a growing number of trustworthy Web sites that subject such clever and deliberate distortions to professional scrutiny. The first, **FactCheck.org**, (www.factcheck.org) was launched at the University of Pennsylvania in 2003. It now has a humorous companion site **FlackCheck.org** (www.flackcheck.org) devoted to spoofing political ads and pointing out errors in political speeches and debates. Other fact-checking organizations followed Factcheck.org in response to the 2004 "Swift Boat" political ads targeting Sen. John Kerry during his run for president. In a sign of their acceptance in the world of journalism, **PolitiFact.com** (www.politifact.com), operated by the *Tampa Bay Times*, won the Pulitzer Prize for its "Truth-O-Meter" ratings of politicians' claims in 2009.

Snopes.com, FactCheck.org and PolitiFact.com all operate at the national level. So does Glenn Kessler's **Fact Checker** (www.washingtonpost.com/blogs/fact-checker) column at the *Washington Post*, which grades the seriousness of falsehoods by awarding from one to four "Pinocchios." The Associated Press has fact-checked politician's claims since 1993, as part of the coverage it offers affiliated news media. Another resource at the national level is **Keeping Them Honest** (http://ac360.blogs.cnn.com/category/keeping-them-honest/), a regular feature on Anderson Cooper's news program "360" on CNN. A *New York Times* affiliate company, About.com, also debunks false claims, photos and videos at **UrbanLegends.about.com** (http://urbanlegends.about.com/). Questionable medical claims are reviewed at **QuackWatch.org** (http://quackwatch.org/).

More recently fact-checking operations have begun at the state and metropolitan level.[11] PolitiFact has entered partnerships with newspapers in Florida, Georgia, New Jersey, Ohio, Oregon, Rhode Island, Texas, Virginia and Wisconsin. It expected to have outlets in all 50 states beginning in 2012. (To find PolitiFact's state fact-checking sites visit PolitiFact.com and mouse over the "PolitiFact National" button at the top of the page, then click on the appropriate state.)

A number of regional news media have instituted their own fact-checking operations. Focusing on Arizona is **AZ Fact Check**, a partnership among the *Arizona Republic*, Phoenix 12 News and the Cronkite School of Journalism and Mass Communication at Arizona State University. **PoliGraph**, a partnership between Minnesota Public Radio and the Humphrey Institute of Public Affairs at the University of

Minnesota checks political fact claims in that state. Other regional fact-checking sites include the *Denver Post's* **Political Polygraph**, the *Tacoma* (Washington) *Tribune's* **Political Smell Test**, the **Voice of San Diego's fact-check blog, BamaFactCheck.com**, operated by the *Anniston* (Alabama) *Star*, and the *Seattle Times* **Truth Needle**.

These sites are easy to find on the Web. Just enter the bold-faced name above into a search engine such as Google. The fact-check sites are themselves searchable by entering the title or gist of a political claim you want to check. They also vet political speeches, ads and quotes in news media in an ongoing attempt to hold politicians accountable. And some will allow you to submit claims you'd like them to check. Collectively they represent an antidote to some of the poison in the infosphere.

In addition to Web sites dedicated to checking facts, there are various groups across the political spectrum that monitor news media performance including bias. Here are a few: On the left, there's Media Matters for America (www.mediamatters.org) and FAIR (Fairness and Accuracy in Reporting at www.fair.org), toward the center lie *Columbia Journalism Review* (www.cjr.org), *American Journalism Review* (www.ajr.org) and NPR's On the Media (www.onthemedia.org), and to the right you'll find AIM (Accuracy in Media, at www.aim.org), and the Media Research Center (www.mrc.org). (Disclosure: I subscribe to *Columbia Journalism Review* and contribute to On the Media.)

3. The Internet puts a virtual reference library at our fingertips 24/7, enabling us to conduct our own fact-checks

The more you know, the less likely you are to be fooled. Here's how the Internet can help you find reliable consumer information, helpful advice, news and facts with just a few keystrokes.

Consumer information

Not all advertising is biased; price information is often reliable, partly because it's against the law to lie or mislead people about what products cost. But the motivation is always to persuade you to buy (now!) and often to convince you that mere *wants* are really *needs*. Fortunately, the Web now provides consumer evaluations on a wide variety of goods and services.

ConsumerReports.org is the source with a perfect PIE chart — Its **P**roximate — testing products in its own labs and reporting first-hand on the results. It's **I**ndependent, accepting nothing from companies whose goods it evaluates, declining even advertising to avoid any conflict of interest. And its **E**xpertise is unparalleled. Unfortunately, you have to pay a small annual fee to subscribe. Of course, you can look up products for free in *Consumer Reports* magazine, which is carried by almost every public library. (Disclosure: I subscribe to this magazine.)

Amazon.com is a much newer resource that doesn't conduct any of its own evaluations, but allows customers to review products, giving them from one to five stars. Since Amazon sells an amazing variety of appliances and consumer goods, you can get some idea of how pleased customers have been for many purchases. And the service is free. **AngiesList.com**, another subscription service, carries ratings of local service providers – painters, roofers, plumbers, contractors and the like, even doctors and dentists. These are submitted by customers and monitored by AngiesList to avoid companies stuffing the ballot box for their own services or to "dis" competitors. (Disclosure: I subscribe to this service.) **Cnet.com** provides free evaluations of high tech consumer goods like laptops, TVs, cameras and smart phones. **Yelp.com** carries free customer evaluations of local restaurants and other retailers and provides a map that makes it easy to find what you're looking for.

Be careful. All ratings systems that rely on consumer evaluations are susceptible to false reviews.[12] Yelp has been criticized for this vulnerability. David Segal, author of the *New York Times* blog, The Haggler, wrote: "As a consumer review Web site, Yelp is so big and influential that it has given rise to a small, semi-underground group of entrepreneurs who, for a fee, will post a rave about your company. Others will post a negative review about your rivals."[13] According to Mr. Segal, Yelp has been refining its automated filtering system in an attempt to thwart such fraudulent reviews with mixed results. By the way, Mr. Segal does *not* endorse consumer evaluations conducted by the Chamber of Commerce's Better Business Bureau.[14] They are not independent.

Online advice

The number of Web sites providing instructions for home or automotive repair, advice about gardening, investing, health, etc. grows daily. To find them, simply type the keywords "[topic] advice" into a Google or other search engine. Try to find Web sites that are affiliated with universities (whose Web addresses end in .edu) or government agencies (.gov). Sites affiliated with reputable news organizations such as NPR, the *New York Times, Wall Street Journal, Washington Post, Los Angeles Times* and other major metro newspapers carry the imprimatur of those companies. In contrast, sites like the Drudge Report ("Wife Cuts Husband's Manhood, Throws in Garbage Disposal") or the Huffington Post[15] ("Naked woman with gun storms motel lobby: Cops"), lack such editorial standards. Remember that search engines don't order the list of Web sites they provide by quality or integrity, but simply by mechanical algorithms that try to guess what you want from the search words entered. To avoid being fooled, always apply the SMELL test.

News

Nutritionists say you become what you eat: It's healthy to vary your diet, but go easy on the junk food. I'd urge the same for your informational diet, and for the same reason. Diversify your news and information sources, but avoid the shouters on all sides. Fox News breaks some important stories you won't hear on NPR or PBS, and vice versa. So does Democracy Now on the left side of the FM dial and on cable. For depth on breaking news, magazines such as *The Atlantic, The Economist, The National Review, The New Yorker, The Weekly Standard, Mother Jones* and *Harpers* are worth perusing.

Although mainstream news media have shriveled in the past decade and their content has become more sensational and less substantive, the national newspapers mentioned above and most major metropolitan papers remain useful, factual sources for general news. When a natural disaster strikes nearby I watch local TV news, but rarely otherwise. Local newscasts scored poorly on our annual analyses of the journalistic quality of local media at Grade the News[16] and national studies show a similar pattern of crime-, sports- and weather-saturated reporting.[17] (Disclosure: I contribute to KQED, my local NPR station, and subscribe to the *New York Times* and *San Jose Mercury News*.)

The public considers my credibility rankings as reliable as shipping cheese by mouse. A 2010 survey conducted by the Pew Research Center rated local TV news as the most believable daily news program with 69 percent giving it positive marks. (This always stuns newspaper people, and even some journalists at local stations.) CNN was next at 65 percent, then ABC News at 64 percent, NBC at 63 percent, CBS at 62 percent, NPR and MSNBC at 60 percent, followed by "your daily newspaper" at 59 percent, the *New York Times* at 58 percent along with C-SPAN, Fox News at 56 percent (and also the highest percent who "believe almost nothing" at 22 percent) and *USA Today* at 56 percent. PBS was not rated.[18]

Access to the Web sites of most of these news organizations named above is free as I write this, but soon you may have to pay for more than occasional access.

Conducting our own fact-checks.

If a fact-claim you wish to investigate has not been addressed on any of the fact-checking sites mentioned above, the Web now makes do-it-yourself vetting possible without spending the day in a research library. Skillful use of search engines and certain reference Web sites are key.

While natural language searches, where you type in a question, are still to be perfected, it's possible to fashion *key word phrases* to get at answers. Suppose you wanted to check a claim by a politician that the Health Care Reform Act of 2010 will cost the government more than it will save. When I entered "cost of health care reform act" in Google, the fourth item listed on the first page of results was an analysis from the Congressional Budget Office. As a source, the CBO has a nearly perfect PIE score — it's a group of expert, non-partisan analysts who study the economics of policy proposals before Congress.

In the second paragraph, I saw this sentence: "CBO and the staff of the Joint Committee on Taxation (JCT) estimate that enacting both pieces of legislation will produce a net reduction in federal deficits of $143 billion over the 2010-2019 period." Checking this fact claim took less than three minutes.

Another resource worth mentioning is **Google Scholar** (http://scholar.google.com/schhp?hl=en&tab=ns or navigate to Scholar from the "More" tab at the top of the Google home page). It provides access to abstracts and sometimes full texts of studies conducted by university researchers in many fields. There are two drawbacks. The writing is often as stiff as an octogenarian at daybreak. And because of the review process, the data lag current events by at least a year. On the other hand, peer review tends to enhance their credibility.

A third national resource is **Times Topics** at the *New York Times* (http://topics.nytimes.com/topics/reference/timestopics/index.html?src=hp1-0-T). In its own words, "Each topic page collects all the news, reference and archival information, photos, graphics, audio and video files published on topics ranging from Madonna to Myanmar. This treasure trove is available without charge on articles going back to 1981."

Going to the morgue

When I was a reporter, the first thing I would do after being assigned a story was to head for the "morgue." Most newspapers scissored their daily product to ribbons and stuffed all of the stories about a particular person or issue into an envelope. They were arranged alphabetically in the newspaper library. It was a terrific way to background yourself on just about any local topic.

Those "dead" articles have now been digitized so reporters can call them up on their screens without leaving their desks. So can you. So should you, if you want to get smart quickly about local civic issues or people. Most news media clip files are searchable online. You can either click on the "archive" button — usually in a tool bar across the top of the screen or a set of options in the right or left margin — or there's a "search" box near the top of the opening screen of whichever newspaper you are searching. Not only can you see the original reporting, but you can follow the development of an issue over time. Most newspapers also append corrections to their own reporting so you won't be misled by a mistake in the original. These files are invaluable in holding leaders to account because you can read what they said in the past and compare it with present positions and actions. You need not rely on Jon Stewart to expose contradiction and hypocrisy.

Other Web resources

Wikipedia.org is a great place to *start* a background search on almost any topic. Lately, it also covers breaking news. It has been widely criticized for inaccuracy since anyone can write or edit its entries. But since 2005, it has taken precautions against false content by requiring citations to other published materials. It's not an ironclad defense against manipulation or falsehood, but has improved its reputation. While it's not a definitive source, Wikipedia can provide a capsule view that can later be checked against more authoritative sources.

By applying the SMELL test, you can assemble a collection of news providers and commentators that you trust. Here are a few suggestions compiled by Christopher Callahan and Leslie-Jean Thornton of the Walter Cronkite School of Journalism and Mass Communication at Arizona State University, along with a few of my own nominations:

General Facts

InfoPlease.com combines an almanac, dictionary and the Columbia Encyclopedia.

Publicagenda.org provides non-partisan background on key public issues from crime to education to environment to health care to social security.

Census.gov/compendia/statab provides a wealth of statistics about the U.S. population from agriculture to wholesale and retail trade compiled by the U.S. Census Bureau.

The World Factbook (https://www.cia.gov/library/publications/the-world-factbook/index.html.) describes itself this way: "provides information on the history, people, government, economy, geography, communications, transportation, military, and transnational issues for 267 world entities."

The New York Times Newsroom Navigator (http://topics.nytimes.com/top/news/technology/cyber timesnavigator/index.html/index.html) provides an extraordinary list of hundreds of reference Web sites used by reporters at the *Times*.

Politics

Project Vote Smart (www.votesmart.org) advertises itself as "The voter's self-defense system." It reports on the voting records and positions of both national and state candidates for office, campaign finances, "political courage," and the ratings of candidates by special interest groups from abortion rights to environment issues to gun rights to women's issues. (Disclosure: I've contributed to this project.) The project's nifty new Vote Easy Web site won the 2011 Webvisionary Award. It allows you to compare your stance on major public questions with every candidate running for national office that you are entitled to vote for based on where you live. The candidates who agree with you come forward on the page and those who disagree remain in the background. It looks like this:

Thomas (http://thomas.loc.gov) named for Thomas Jefferson and maintained by the Library of Congress, it contains vast amounts of well-organized information about all U.S. House and Senate legislation, the *Congressional Record*, email and postal addresses for legislators, founding documents like the Constitution and much more. It's searchable by bill text, topic and number. You can also browse bills sponsored by any legislator.

Fedstats.gov provides links to statistics from more than 100 federal agencies.

General Accounting Office (www.gao.gov) is the investigative arm of Congress and makes its reports public online within days of providing the information to legislators.

Opinion Polls

Gallup (www.gallup.com) is one of the oldest national polling organizations and one of the more trusted.

Roper (www.ropercenter.uconn.edu) also does reputable polling on public issues.

Pew Research Center for People and the Press (www.people-press.org) provides quality polls on politics and press issues.

Because polling is as much art as science, it's always wise to aggregate several polls asking similar questions and take the mean, or average, of their results. It's risky to rely on a single poll's numbers. Also recognize that pollsters push people to offer opinions about things they know little about. Such opinions are unstable and likely to change.

Health

National Center for Health Statistics (www.cdc.gov/nchs) provides information about public health and various diseases.

U.S. Food and Drug Administration (www.fda.gov) provides useful alerts and information about the safety of the food supply and medicine.

U.S. Consumer Product Safety Commission (www.cpsc.gov) evaluates a variety of consumer goods for threats to health or safety.

Science

The **National Academy of Sciences (http://www.nationalacademies.org/)** bills itself as "where the nation turns for Independent, expert advice." You can access and search more than 4,000 scientific reports on a wide variety of scientific issues from earthquake preparedness to adverse effects of vaccines, all for free.

The **American Society for the Advancement of Science** (**www.aaas.org/**) publishes the magazine *Science* and provides free policy statements on most of the controversial public issues of the day.

Crime

FBI Uniform Crime Reports (www.fbi.gov/ucr/ucr. htm) provides a wealth of national and state data on numbers and trends of various types of crime.

National Criminal Justice Reference Service (www.ncjrs.gov) provides in-depth information about corrections, juvenile justice, courts, crime prevention, victims, etc.

Environment

U.S. Environmental Protection Agency (www.epa. gov) provides information on topics from acid rain to drinking water to pesticides to UV index to waste.

4. Social media allow us to collaborate in vetting content with others who may be more knowledgeable

"The ecology of knowledge has filled out. The ability of people to engage in discussions and to get additive knowledge and perspectives is orders ... of magnitude better than it was."[19]

~ David Weinberger, senior researcher at Harvard's Berkman Center for Internet and Society

One of the newest ways to avoid being fooled is to ask your friends and colleagues on a social network like **Facebook, Linked-In** or **Twitter** to respond to a fact-claim or whole article. Collectively our professional and friendship networks have vastly greater knowledge than we do as individuals. Fact-checking is naturally a social activity.

There is also a Web site to facilitate such networking. **NewsTrust.net** (www.newstrust.net) has created tools that allow anyone to nominate a news article on the Web for analysis by themselves and other raters. The site then makes the evaluation and the article available for everyone. (A disclosure and a caveat: I helped set up the news evaluation system for this site; and its status is uncertain due to lack of fresh funding.)

5. The Web can even help us discover people and perspectives that are ignored or marginalized in mainstream U.S. media

One of the greatest blessings of the Internet has been the ability of previously voiceless people to put their viewpoints before the public, to emerge from the silence. But the Web doesn't merely give voice to the voiceless, it allows us a multiperspectival view of news that would have been impossible even for someone with access to the world's greatest library in 1990. With a few keystrokes you can find alternate reports about the same events and issues, not just on international and national stories, but on the state and metro levels.

Absent the Internet, the average American citizen would have had to settle for a handful of news reports about the efforts of a group of activists in the summer of 2011 to sail from Greece to Gaza carrying humanitarian aid and protesting the Israeli blockade of Gaza. All would have reflected an American point of view. But a Google News search requiring a tenth of a second made 3,340 articles available from around the world presenting a wide array of viewpoints from a *Jerusalem Post* article quoting an Israeli official claiming that the presence of fund-raiser for HAMAS among the activists "is clear proof that this is not a humanitarian flotilla, but a provocation and a terror operation in disguise of a flotilla,"[20] to an Al-Jazeera op-ed arguing that "that the deadly influence of Israeli special interests groups on Western governments, especially that of the USA, means that advocates of justice for the Palestinians have only one recourse: civil society actions such as the Gaza humanitarian flotillas."[21] In between were reports and commentaries about the flotillas from around the Globe. A Yahoo News search generated 3,369 articles. Bing News presented 5,890 articles. The fact that many of the articles are written in languages other than English presents little problem. Both Yahoo (babelfish.yahoo.com) and Google (translate.google.com) can translate a block of text or an entire Web site almost instantly for free. Such computerized translations don't measure up to a professional's work, but do allow the reader to capture the gist of an article.

Travel abroad provides a wider and wiser perspective on the U.S. and life in general, but airfare and hotels are expensive. You can gain a global point-of-view reading the news on foreign Web sites at little or no cost. I've placed a list of international news sources reporting in English in the notes for this chapter at the end of the book.[22]

Moving from the international to national to state and local, the number of articles diminishes because there are fewer journalists or parajournalists (citizen journalists, bloggers, etc.) covering them. As you narrow your search geographically, it's helpful to use the "advanced search" option Google offers.[23] For example, when I entered "Ohio state budget bill" in a basic Google News search about a month after it passed at the end of June, 2011, some 2,300 articles turned up. But many were about the federal budget debt ceiling debate rather than Ohio's budget. The advanced search function allowed me to eliminate the federal stories and focus just on Ohio media.

By eliminating irrelevant articles I was able to reduce my search to just 140 articles from the *Cleveland Plain Dealer's* mainstream coverage ("Gov. John Kasich signs two-year state budget, but vetoes seven items first") to a YouTube video of

Dayton station WDTN's report ("Concealed weapons allowed in bars") to *The Independent Collegian*'s article about how the new budget would affect tuition at the University of Toledo ("FY12 budget brings increases in tuition and residence hall costs"). Those 140 articles contained a much wider range of topics related to the state budget than the media available anywhere in Ohio before the Web.

Unfortunately, the consolidation of mainstream media at the regional and metro level has shrunk the number of independent professional journalists reporting on local issues and events. When I entered the term "city budget" in Google News advanced search and limited it to articles about San Jose, CA, during the month after the budget passed, 21 articles appeared, two-thirds of which concerned cities other than San Jose. (Obviously, Google's search engine is far from perfect!) The remaining articles almost all came from just one source, the *San Jose Mercury News.*

A final word

We are living through as profound a period of change in our information environment as humans have ever experienced. And it's happening much more quickly than in past communication revolutions. The ability to identify reliable news and information in the digital age is essential not just for individuals, but for the whole society. Governments can require corporations to reduce pollution of the atmosphere, but the First Amendment renders the government powerless against most pollution in the infosphere. It's up to us. The eminent newspaper columnist Walter Lippmann's warning is as relevant today as when he wrote it in 1920:

> All that the sharpest critics of democracy have alleged is true if there is no steady supply of trustworthy and relevant news. Incompetence and aimlessness, corruption and disloyalty, panic and ultimate disaster must come to any people which is denied assured access to the facts. No one can manage anything on pap. Neither can a people.[24]

Notes

Ch. 1: The Age of Transformative Information Paradoxes

1. The Knight Commission on the Information Needs of Communities in a Democracy (2009) *Informing communities: Sustaining democracy in the digital age,* "Executive Summary," Washington, DC: Aspen Institute, p. 1, online at http://www.knightcomm.org /executive-summary/.

2. Pingdom, (1/12/2011) "Internet 2010 in Numbers," online at http://royal.pingdom.com/2011/01/12/internet-2010-in-numbers/).

3. Anne Mintz, Ed. (2002) *Web of deception: Misinformation on the internet,* Medford, NJ: CyberAge Books. Or visit ConsumerWebWatch.org for an updated source of misinformation on the Web.

4. A.J. Liebling (1975) *The press,* Pantheon: New York, p. 32. Originally published May 14, 1960 in *The New Yorker* column, "The wayward press," under the title, "Do you belong in journalism?"

5. Project for Excellence in Journalism (2012) *The state of the news media: 2011,* online at: http://stateofthemedia.org/.

6. Jan Schaffer (2007) *Citizen media: Fad or the future of news?* Knight Citizen News Network, online at: http://www.kcnn.org/research/citizen_media_report.

7. Andrew Keen, author of *The cult of the amateur* told the *Washington Post:* Journalists "follow a set of standards, a code of ethics. Objectivity rules. That's not the case with citizen journalists. Anything goes in that world." See Jose Antonio Vargas (11/27/2007) "Storming the news gatekeepers on the internet, citizen journalists raise their voices," *Washington Post,* p. C1.

8. Research about journalism conducted partly or mostly by citizens has consistently been shown to be unequal to that in traditional media, especially newspapers. For example, in 2010 Prof. Frederick Fico and colleagues at Michigan State University conducted a scientific national study of citizen journalism Web sites and compared them to local daily and weekly newspapers in the same community on the quantity and quality of their coverage of local government. His team found that the citizen sites were no substitute for newspaper coverage and that coverage of local government was rare in all but large cities. See Frederick Fico, Stephen Lacy, Thomas Baldwin, Daniel Bergan, Steven S. Wildman and Paul Zube (2011) "Citizen journalism sites as information substitutes and complements for newspaper coverage of local governments," in press. Also see *Citizen media: Fad or the future of news?* cited above.

For a more optimistic portrait of non-traditional news media, see Dan Gillmor's self-published 2010 book, *Mediactive.*

9. Brooke Gladstone (6/17/2011) "FCC report says local reporting in crisis," On the Media, National Public Radio, online at http://www.onthemedia.org/transcripts/2011/06/17/04.

10. Paul Farhi (Spring, 2010) "Lost in the woods: Sinking standards, the media and Tiger Woods," *American Journalism Review*, pp. 14-19. The falling standards of mainstream news media will be covered in detail in chapter 4.

11. Steven Waldman (2011) *Information needs of communities: The changing media landscape in a broadband age*, Washington, DC: Federal Communication Commission, available online and for download at: http://www.fcc.gov/info-needs-communities.

12. Ken Auletta (3/17/2011) presentation at Stony Brook University's School of Journalism, online at http://vimeo.com/21992631.

13. Ben Zimmer (2/13/2011) "How the war of words was won," *New York Times,* Week in Review, p. 4. Also see Nicholas D. Kristof, (2/13/2011) "What Egypt can teach America," *New York Times,* Week in Review, p. 10.

14. Bill Moyers (2/17/2012) "Decoding the campaign," interview with Kathleen Hall Jamieson on Moyers and Company, Public

Affairs Television, available online at: http://billmoyers.com/episode/full-show-decoding-the-campaigns/.

15. Amy Goodman (5/27/2011) Democracy Now, interview with Eli Pariser, author of *The Filter Bubble*, online at: http://www.democracynow.org /2011/5/27/eli_pariser_on_the_filter_bubble.

16. Goodman, cited above.

17. Cordelia Fine (8/31/2011) "Biased but brilliant," *New York Times*, Sunday Review, p. 12.

18. Joe Nocera (12/18/2010) "Explaining the crisis with dogma," Talking business column, *New York Times*, p. B1. Other evidence of partisanship: According to *Newsweek* (8/15/2011), in the 1960s, 8% of major bills faced a filibuster. By 2011, the proportion increased to 70%, making it difficult to pass any bill without 60 of 100 senators voting for it; "8 ways to fix our politics," pp. 22-23.

19. Rush Limbaugh (1/11/2009) The Rush Limbaugh Show, online at: http://www.youtube.com/watch?v=c-87ymLU96E.

20. Union of Concerned Scientists, "Global Warming," online at: http://www.ucsusa.org/global_warming/. (Disclosure: I have contributed to the Union of Concerned Scientists.)

21. National surveys conducted by the Pew Research Center for the People and the Press showed that 79% of Americans believed there was "solid evidence the earth is warming" in 2006, but only 59% agreed in Oct. 2010. In 2010, 79% of Democrats agreed, but only 38% of Republicans. Only 30% of Republicans agreed that scientists have reached consensus on global warming vs. twice as many Democrats. See Pew Research Center (10/27/2010) "Wide partisan divide over global warming," online at: http://pewresearch.org/pubs/1780/poll-global-warming-scientists-energy-policies-offshore-drilling-tea-party.

22. James Madison, "Federalist Paper No. 62" in Clinton Rossiter, Ed. (2000, orig. 1822) *The Federalist Papers*, New York: Signet Classic.

23. Wikipedia, (undated) "The Battle of New Orleans," accessed 7/15/2011 online at: http://en.wikipedia.org/wiki/Battle_of_New_Orleans.

24. Joseph E. Stiglitz and Linda J. Bilmes (2008) *The three-trillion dollar war*, New York: W.W. Norton.

25. Amy Goodman and Juan Gonzalez (1/12/2012) Democracy Now, interview Michael Copps.

26. Bill Moyers (9/12/08) Bill Moyers Journal, Public Broadcasting System, interview with Brooke Gladstone, online at http://www.pbs.org/moyers/journal/09122008/watch2.html. Ms. Gladstone is the co-host of NPR's On the Media.

Ch. 2: Truth vs. Truthiness

1. Stephen Colbert (1/10/2007) The Colbert Report, online at http://www.gametrailers.com/user-move/truthiness-the-colbert-report/33403.

2. Politifact.com (5/2011) "Truth-o-meter: Jon Kyl says abortion services are 'well over 90 percent of what Planned Parenthood does,'" *St. Petersburg Times*, online at: http://www.politifact.com/truth-o-meter/statements/2011/apr/08/jon-kyl/jon-kyl-says-abortion-services-are-well-over-90-pe/.

3. Molecular Expressions, "Optical microscopy primer: basics of light and color," available online at: http://micro.magnet.fsu.edu/primer/lightandcolor/electromagintro.html.

4. Robert Ornstein (2008) *MindReal: How the mind creates its own virtual reality*, Boston: Malor Books, p. 106.

5. In this paragraph and the next I'm relying on Daniel Kahneman (2011) *Thinking, fast and slow*, New York: Farrar, Straus and Giroux; Richard H. Thaler and Cass R. Sunstein (2008) *Nudge: Improving decisions about health, wealth, and happiness*, New York: Penguin; and George Lakoff (2008) *The political mind: Why you can't understand 21st-century American politics with an 18th-century brain*, New York: Viking Press.

6. I know many of you have been warned about trusting Wikipedia. After 2005 it changed its rules for contributors requiring that they cite published materials and barring original research. More recently

it's been accused of being too restrictive, requiring too extensive use of footnotes (Noam Cohen, 8/8/2011, "When knowledge isn't written, does it still count?" *New York Times*, p. B4.) I use Wikipedia here only after checking elsewhere. I include it where I think it's reliable because it's online, so with just a click you can go deeper if you're curious. Here's more on atoms, http://en.wikipedia.org/wiki/Atom#History and subatomic particles: http://en.wikipedia.org/wiki/List_of_particles.

7. Michael Krasny (6/22/2010) Forum, KQED-FM, interview with journalist and author Kathryn Schulz author of *Being Wrong: Adventures in the Margin of Error*.

8. I adapted this example from Earl Babbie (2007) *The practice of social research*, 11th ed., Belmont, CA: Thomson Wadsworth.

Ch. 3: Where Does Bias Come From?

1. Albert H. Hastorf and Hadley Cantril (1971, original 1954) "They saw a game: A case study," in Wilbur F. Schramm and Donald F. Roberts, Eds. *The process and effects of mass communication*, second edition, Urbana, IL: University of Illinois Press, pp. 300-312.

2. Hastorf and Cantril, p. 308.

3. Ashleigh Banfield (4/29/2003) "MSNBC's Banfield slams war coverage," Alternet, online at: http://www.alternet.org/story/15778.

4. Robert Ornstein (2008) *MindReal: How the mind creates its own virtual reality*, Boston: Malor Books. Dr. Ornstein is a cognitive scientist at Stanford University.

5. Malcolm Gladwell (2005) *Blink*, New York: Little, Brown and Company, p. 223.

6. Jack Glaser (2007) "The social psychology of intergroup bias, summary of concepts and research," online at: http://calswec.berkeley.edu/calswec/2007_FE_SocialPsychPrejudic e.pdf. Dr. Glaser is a professor at the Goldman School of Public Policy, University of California, Berkeley.

7. Max H. Bazerman and Ann E. Tenbrunsel (2011) *Blind spots: why we fail to do what's right and what to do about it,* Princeton, NJ: Princeton University Press.

8. Max H. Bazerman and Ann E. Tenbrunsel (4/21/2011) "Stumbling into bad behavior," *New York Times,* op-ed, p. A21, online at:
http://www.nytimes.com/2011/04/21/opinion/21bazerman.html?_r=1&scp=1&sq=%22Stumbling%20into%20bad%20behavior%22&st=cse.

Even scientists — those paragons of dispassionate rationality — have to guard against the power of self-interest to distort their perceptions. To be published in a scientific journal, research must be vetted by peers. In many journals, those who fund the research now must be named as a hedge against unconscious or willful tailoring of results to please sponsors. To be accepted as knowledge, studies must be replicated by others. So powerful and subconscious is the influence of self-interest, medical science has adopted as its gold standard "double-blind" experiments in which not even the researcher know which pill is the placebo and which the actual medicine until the study is complete.

9. Robert Maynard's daughter, Dori, carries on his work at the Maynard Institute for Education in Journalism in Oakland. In 2006 she held a question and answer session with editors to explain fault lines analysis. See: http://www.editteach.org/special/editingthefuture/06_Maynard/video01.htm.

10. Bill Moyers (2/3/2012) "How do conservatives and liberals see the world?" interview with Jonathan Haidt, Moyers and Company, Public Affairs Television Inc., available online at:
http://billmoyers.com/episode/how-do-conservatives-and-liberals-see-the-world/.

11. George Gallup, Ed. (1998) *The Gallup Poll: Public Opinion, 1997,* Lanham, MD: Rowman and Littlefield Publishing Group; available online at:
http://books.google.com/books?id=fLGQKjdXJCsC&pg=PA23&lpg=PA23&dq=%22oj+simpson%22+and+public+reaction+of+blacks+and+whites&source=web&ots=jmNzrZcsEq&sig=VAi0XxF3oPt0lfuyN6IAH9nemSw#PPA22,M1.

12. Anthony Lewis (10/6/1995) "Abroad at home; an American dilemma," *New York Times*; available online at: http://query.nytimes.com/gst/fullpage.html?res=9A0DE4DE1239 F935A35753C1A963958260.

13. Karen Grigsby Bates (10/3/2005) "The O.J. Simpson Verdict, Race and the Media," on Day to Day, National Public Radio; available online at: http://www.npr.org/templates/story/story.php?storyId=4934067.

14. Dennis Gilbert (1998). *The American class structure*, New York: Wadsworth Publishing.

15. Pew Charitable Trusts Economic Mobility Project (11/2011) "Does America promote mobility as well as other nations?" available online at: http://www.economicmobility.org/reports_and_research/other?id =0017.

16. William Thompson and Joseph Hickey (2005) *Society in focus*, Boston: Pearson.

17. Youth Media Council (since renamed the Center for Media Justice) (2007) "Displacing the dream," online at http://www.datacenter.org/displacing-the-dream/. Also at: http://209.85.173.104/search?q=cache:XtmxU8OQHzUJ:cmj.cente rformediajustice.org/documents/download/61+%22Displacing+th e+Dream%22&hl=en&ct=clnk&cd=3&gl=us.

18. Just look at the labels in your clothes, on the back of your computer, or on the frame of your car. Or count the number of nations in the world where U.S. soldiers are garrisoned. Or listen to the accent of the technical support person who assists you by telephone.

19. Phillip Knightly (1975) *The first casualty: From the Crimea to Vietnam – the war correspondent as hero, propagandist and myth maker*, New York: Harcourt Brace Jovanovich.

20. John H. McManus (12/18/2003) "The newsworthiness of death," GradeTheNews.org, online at: http://www.gradethenews.org/pages/middleeast.htm.

21. McManus, cited above.

22. Deborah Tannen (1990) *You just don't understand: Women and men in conversation*, New York: Ballantine Books, pp. 24-25. In the 1980s feminist scholars such as Carol Gilligan showed that research on moral development and ethics based entirely on male subjects was misleading and incomplete because of gender differences. See, for example, Professor Gilligan's path-breaking 1982 book *In a different voice*, Cambridge, MA: Harvard University Press.

23. Tannen, p. 241.

24. Nicholas Kristof (2/10/08) "When women rule," *New York Times*, online at: http://www.nytimes.com/2008/02/10 /opinion/10kristof.html_ r=1&hp&oref=slogin.

25. Kim Barker (2/20/2011) "Why we need women in war zones," *New York Times*, Week in Review, p. 11.

26. Michael Krasny (3/23/2011)Forum, KQED-FM, interview with David Brooks about his 2011 book *The social animal: The hidden sources of love, character, and achievement*, New York: Random House.

27. John Tierney (2/7/2011) "Social scientist sees bias within," *New York Times*, p. D1, online at: http://www.nytimes.com/2011/02/ 08/ science /08tier.html?scp=1&sq=%22liberal%20bias%22&st= cse.

Ch. 4: The Covert Bias of Institutions

1. Robert M. Hutchins and the Commission on Freedom of the Press (1947) *A free and responsible press: a general report on mass communication: newspapers, radio, motion pictures, magazines, and books.* (Chicago: University of Chicago Press) p. 57. After World War II, *Time* magazine founder Henry Luce commissioned University of Chicago President Robert M. Hutchins to assemble some of the best thinkers in the nation to consider the role of the press in a democracy. The result was a slim but remarkable book that defined what's come to be known as "socially responsible journalism." By the way, media moguls, including Mr. Luce, loathed the report.

2. Tommy Tomlinson (5/15/2011) "A team tackles brown lung disease, wins a Pulitzer Prize," the *Charlotte Observer*, available online at: http://www.charlotteobserver.com/2011/05/11/2280312/a-team-tackles-brown-lung-disease.html#storylink=cpy.

3. Project for Excellence in Journalism (1/11/2010) "How news happens—still: A study of the news ecosystem of Baltimore," available online at http://pewresearch.org/pubs/1458/news-changing-media-baltimore.

4. On Aug. 18, 1896 Adolph Ochs wrote in a signed editorial after he took over ownership of the paper, "It will be my earnest aim that the New York Times ... give the news impartially, without fear or favor, regardless of party, sect, or interest involved." The entire editorial is available online at: http://www.nytimes.com/1996/08/19/opinion/without-fear-or-favor.html. "Fair and balanced" is a trademarked slogan of the Fox News Channel. Wikipedia (accessed 8/8/2011) Fox News Channel, online at: http://en.wikipedia.org/wiki/Fox_News_Channel.

5. Steve Inskeep (5/13/2011) Morning Edition, National Public Radio. Quote is in introduction to Elizabeth Blair's story, "With billions at stake, firms play name that mop."

6. This is most evident in the codes of ethics of journalism, which most commercial news outlets embrace or use as a model for their own codes. The Society of Professional Journalists' code, for example, begins: "Members of the Society of Professional Journalists believe that public enlightenment is the forerunner of justice and the foundation of democracy. The duty of the journalist is to further those ends by seeking truth and providing a fair and comprehensive account of events and issues." The Radio Television Digital News Association declares: "Professional electronic journalists should operate as trustees of the public, seek the truth, report it fairly and with integrity and independence, and stand accountable for their actions."

7. John H. McManus (1997) "Who's responsible for journalism?" *Journal of Mass Media Ethics*, 12, 1 pp. 5-17. Also see Theodore L. Glasser (1986) "Press responsibility and First Amendment values," in Deni Elliott, Ed., *Responsible Journalism*, Thousand Oaks, CA: Sage. In 1947 the Commission on Freedom of the Press wrote: "No public service is more important that the service of communications.

But the element of personal responsibility, which is the essence of the organizations of such professions as law and medicine, is missing in communications. Here the writer works for an employer, and the employer, not the writer takes the responsibility." (p. 77).

8. Conrad C. Fink (1995) *Media Ethics*, Boston: Allyn and Bacon, p. 91.

9. John H. McManus (1995) "A market-based model of news production," *Communication Theory* 5, 4, pp. 301-338.

10. I'm relying here on my previous research which culminated in the following book: John H. McManus (1994) *Market-driven journalism: Let the citizen beware?* Thousand Oaks, CA: Sage.

11. In his book *Newsonomics*, Ken Doctor puts it this way: "Consider the travails of *The New York Times*... One day last April it won five Pulitzer Prizes. The next day, it suffered the indignity of announcing the biggest quarterly loss in its history -- $74 million." Ken Doctor (2010) *Newsonomics*, New York: St. Martin's Press.

12. Steven D. Reese (1991) "Setting the media's agenda: A power balance perspective," in James A. Anderson, Ed., *Communication Yearbook 14*, Newbury Park, CA: Sage, pp. 309-340. Frank Fitzpatrick, a sports writer for the *Philadelphia Inquirer* provided a case in point in a conversation with Bob Garfield of NPR's On the Media: When asked what would happen if Fitzpatrick had revealed the sleazy side of Phillies baseball star Lenny Dykstra's life, he responded "Behind everything a baseball beat writer does there's this fear of severing a good relationship [with a source] because without them, in a competitive news environment, you're dead." Had he written candidly about Dykstra's bad behavior, the writer said: "There would have been very few players that would have talked to me. And the manager would have been even more difficult to deal with. You would have been able to do your job, but only in the most routine, uninteresting fashion imaginable. In terms of inside information, you would have been lost." Bob Garfield (7/8/2011) On the Media, National Public Radio.

13. Michele McLellan (3/14/2011) "Emerging economics of community news," *State of the News Media: 2011* Washington, DC: Project for Excellence in Journalism, online at: http://stateofthe media.org/2011/mobile-survey/economics-of-community-news/

14. These trends are evident in the annual reports compiled by the Project for Excellence in Journalism's State of the news media, available online at: www.stateof themedia.org.

15. Douglas McCollam (July/August 2008) "Sulzberger at the barricades," *Columbia Journalism Review*, vol. 48, no. 2, p. 26.

16. John H. McManus (1988) "Economic and technological influences on the quality of local television news," doctoral dissertation, Stanford University.

17. This appears to be changing. In March of 2011 the *New York Times* announced a plan to charge for those who routinely visit its Web site, but are not subscribers to the printed paper. See Jeremy Peters (3/18/2011) "TheTimes announces a digital subscription plan," p. A1. online at: http://www.nytimes.com/2011/03/18/business/media/18times.html?_r=1&ref=todayspaper.

18. Robert G. Picard (2010) *Value Creation and the future of news organizations,* Lisbon, Spain: MediaXXi.

19. Lisa Borenstein (2/27/2009) "Rocky Mountain Bye," *Columbia Journalism Review*, online at http://www.cjr.org/behind_the_news/rocky_ mountain_bye.php?page=all.

20. See, for example, stories awarded the Pulitzer Prize; online at: http://www.pulitzer.org/awards; or http://www.journalism. columbia.edu/cs/ContentServer/jrn/1165270069766/page/117529 5284582/JRNSimplePage2.htm.

21. Ken Auletta (3/17/2011) presentation at Stony Brook University's School of Journalism, online at http://vimeo.com/21992631.

22. Jennifer Dorroh (April/May 2009) "Statehouse exodus," *American Journalism Review*, pp. 20-29.

23. John McManus (10/3/2007) "California leaders decry decline in news quality, particularly state coverage," Grade the News, available online at: http://www.gradethenews.org/2007/decline.htm.

24. Sam McManis (1/15/2008) "Media savvy: NPR's Schorr vital link to 'responsible journalism,'" *Sacramento Bee,* p. 1E, online at: http://www.sacbee.com/107/story/634053.html.

25. Project for Excellence in Journalism (2008) "Overview," *State of the News Media: 2008*, p. 4, available online at: http://www.stateof themedia.org/files/2011/01/PEJ2008-Overview.pdf.

26. Project for Excellence in Journalism (3/17/2008) "The Web: Alarming, appealing and a challenge to journalistic values: Financial woes now overshadow all other concerns for journalists," Pew Research Center for the People and the Press, p. 1; available online at: http://www.stateofthemedia.org/files/2011/01/Journalist-report-2008.pdf.

27. Philip J. Trounstine (4/15/2007) "The crisis of consolidation in Bay Area news media," Grade the News, guest commentary. Trounstine was a long-time political reporter and editor at the *San Jose Mercury News*. His commentary is available at: http://www.gradethenews.org/commentaries/Trounstine.htm.

28. John McManus (6/5/2007) "Inside the Bay Area's newspaper giant," Grade the News. An interview with John Bowman, former editor of the *Daily Review* in Hayward, CA and executive editor of the *San Mateo County Times*. Article available at: http://www.gradethenews.org/2007/bowman.htm.

29. Robert Papper (8/5/2010) "The state of the industry: 2010," study presented at the annual convention of the Association for Education in Journalism and Mass Communication, Denver. Professor Papper of Hofstra University found that only 39% of local television stations did not partner with other local broadcasters or newspapers.

30. Michael Copps, (1/12/2012) interview with Amy Goodman and Juan Gonzalez on Democracy Now, The War and Peace Report.

31. Richard Perez-Pena (11/18/2008) "Web Sites That Dig for News Rise as Watchdogs," *New York Times*, p. A1; available online at: http://www.nytimes.com/2008/11/18/business /media/18voice.html?_r=1&hp.

32. Ken Doctor (3/10/2008) "Regional Dailies Give Business Away," available online at: http://www.contentbridges.com/2008/03/regional-dailie.html.

33. Ted Koppel (3/12/2009) "Do News Providers Live Up to News Literacy Standards?", panel held at Stony Brook University; available online at: http://newsliteracyconference.com/content/?p=498.

34. Jan Schaffer (2007) "Citizen Media: Fad or the Future of News? The rise and prospects of hyperlocal journalism," J-Lab, Knight Community News Network; available online at: http://www.kcnn.org/research/citizen_media_report/.

35. Nick Davies (2009) *Flat Earth News*, London: Vintage Books, p. 16.

36. Gene Roberts and Hank Klibanoff (2006) *The Race Beat: The press, the civil rights struggle, and the awakening of a nation*, New York: Vintage Books. This Pulitzer Prize winning book focuses on the few heroic journalists and brave news organizations that stood up to racial prejudice. Their isolation and what they endured, however, documents the resistance of the regional news media to full and fair reports of the struggle for civil rights in the South. Further examples of pandering to racial and ethnic prejudice can be found in Juan Gonzalez and Joseph Torres (2011) *News for all the people: the epic story of race and the American media*, Brooklyn, NY: Verso Books.

37. Scott McClellan (2008) *What happened: Inside the Bush White House and Washington's culture of deception*, New York: Public Affairs.

38. Brian Stelter (5/30/2008) "Was press a war 'enabler'? Two offer a nod from inside," *New York Times*, p. A17; available online at: http://www.nytimes.com/2008/05/30/washington/30press.html.

39. Bob Garfield (4/29/2011) "Is HuffPost good for journalism?," On the Media, National Public Radio, segment on the Huffington Post. online at: http://www.onthemedia.org/2011/apr/29/is-huffpost-good-for-journalism/transcript/.

40. "Is HuffPost good for journalism?," cited above.

41. Andrew Heyward (3/12/2009) "Do News Providers Live Up to News Literacy Standards?," panel held at Stony Brook University; available online at: http://newsliteracyconference.com/content/?p=498.

42. Karen Stabiner (March/April 2011) "CJR column mentions The Simpsons: a second look at SEO," *Columbia Journalism Review*, pp. 46-48.

43. Thomas C. Leonard (2003) *Mark Twain: Press critic.* Berkeley, CA: University of California Friends of the Bancroft Library. The book features Mark Twain's previously unpublished 1870 essay, "Interviewing the interviewer."

44. McManus, *Market-driven journalism,* previously cited.

45. Deborah Potter (March/April, 2011) "With an edge," *American Journalism Review*, online at: http://www.ajr.org/Article.asp?id=5076.

46. Here are the exact numbers of articles: Tiger Woods (15,400), Nancy Pelosi (10,494), Harry Reid (5,976), Mitch McConnell (3,000) and John Boehner (4,518).

47. Paul Farhi (Spring, 2010) "Lost in the Woods: sinking standards, the media and Tiger Woods," *American Journalism Review*, pp. 14-19.

48. Bill Dwyre (1/19/2008) "Media are off their game," *Los Angeles Times*, p. D1, online at: http://www.latimes.com/sports/la-sp-dwyre19jan19 1,4372597,full.column?coll=la-headlines-sports&ctrack=2&cset=true.

49. Lawrence Lessig (10/25/2011) interviewed on KQED's Forum with Michael Krasny.

50. John McManus (5/5/2005) "Giving readers the finger," GradeTheNews.org, online at: http://www.gradethenews.org/commentaries /finger.htm. What makes this coverage particularly distressing is that it occurred while the *Mercury News* was still run by Knight-Ridder, a chain renowned for quality, and before the worst of newsroom layoffs.

51. Paula Kerger (11/30/2011) interviewed on Forum with Michael Krasny, KQED-FM.

52. Jon Stewart (10/31/2010) "Final speech at the Rally to Restore Sanity in Washington, DC," online at: http://www.youtube.com/watch?v=6JzGOiBXeD4.

53. Tom Rosenstiel, Marion Just, Todd Belt, Atiba Pertilla, Walter Dean, and Dante Chinni (2007) *We interrupt this newscast: How to improve local news and win ratings too*, New York: Cambridge University Press, p. 1.

54. E.J. Dionne (9/3/2009) "The Real Town Hall Story," available online at: http://www.washingtonpost.com/wp-dyn/content/article/2009/09/02/AR2009090202858.html.

55. Bill Watterson (2005) *The complete Calvin and Hobbes*, Kansas City: Andrews McMeel, vol. 3, p. 465.

56. Brian Stelter (12/25/2011) "In Beck's shadow, rise of 'The Five'," *New York Times*, pg. B1, online at http://www.nytimes.com /2011/12/26/business/media/the-five-rises-on-fox-news-in-glenn-becks-shadow.html?sq=Glenn Beck&st=Search&scp= 3&pagewanted=print.

57. Code of Ethics, Society of Professional Journalists, online at: http://spj.org/ethicscode.asp.

58. John McManus (9/13/2005) "SF Examiner and Independent agree to end payola restaurant reviews," Grade the News, online at: http://gradethenews.org/2005/payola.htm. The *Examiner* made a practice of blurring the distinction between news and ads. In a real estate column on July 22, 2005, realtor Bryan Jacobs advised readers to "hire a realtor." His own ad appeared on an adjoining page.

Photo courtesy of Gradethenews.org.

Not only did the *Examiner* write articles to help sell ads, it provided advertisers a chance to write the "news" themselves!

59. Michael Stoll (7/27/2005) "At free dailies, advertisers sometimes call the shots," Grade the News, online at http://www.gradethenews.org/2005/freepapers1.htm.

60. John McManus (9/24/2000) "Is it news or is it advertising?" Grade the News, online at: http://www.gradethenews.org/dreamhost%20files/ pagesfolder/Deception.htm.

61. Michael Stoll (6/20/03) "Running ads as news, the Oakland Tribune's real estate section crosses a journalistic line," online at: http://www.gradethenews.org/pages/news%20as%20ads.htm.

62. Michael Stoll (4/15/2004) "Oakland Tribune pledges end to deceptive 'advertorials'," online at: http://www.gradethenews.org/pages2/advertorial.htm.

63. Michael Stoll (11/21/2005) "Mercury News renounces microscopic ad label," Grade the News, online at: http://www.gradethenews.org/2005 /microads.htm#microads1.

After Grade the News ceased active operation, the *Mercury News* began running similar ads without any advertising label. Here's what the label looked like with a penny for reference:

64. See http://www.gradethenews.org/feat/archives.htm #advertising.

65. John,McManus (9/24/2000) "Is it news or is it advertising?" cited above. The *Contra Costa Times* grudgingly agreed to label the section after our story.

66. James Rainey (9/15/2010) "The news is, that pitch was paid for; When spokespersons for hire promote products on local TV news shows," *Los Angeles Times*, available online at: latimes.com/ entertainment/news/la-et-onthemedia-20100915,0,370372.column. Accessed 9/20/2010.

67. Beats are areas of coverage to which reporters are assigned, for example, city hall, health, police, education, and courts.

68. Joseph Turow (1984) *Media industries*, New York: Longman.

69. See, for example, Bob Butler (5/7/2011) "Fair and unbalanced: the tale of two trials," Maynard Institute for Journalism Education, online at: http://mije.org/health/fair-and-unbalanced-tale-two-trials#comment-2498; and Jean Marie Browne (Fall, 2011) "Familiar Patterns of Minority Exclusion Follow Mainstream Media Online," Nieman Reports, available online at: http://www.nieman.harvard.edu/reports/article/102675/Familiar-

Patterns-of-Minority-Exclusion-Follow-Mainstream-Media-Online.aspx.

70. Arthur S. Brisbane (1/9/2011) "Hanging on as the boundaries shift," *New York Times*, Week in Review, p. 10; available online at: http://www.nytimes.com/2011/01/09/opinion/09pubed.html?scp=16&sq=Arthur+Brisbane&st=nyt.

71. Nick Davies (2009) *Flat Earth News* cited above, p. 60.

72. Steven Waldman (6/17/2011) "FCC report says local reporting in crisis," On the Media, National Public Radio, online at: http://www.onthemedia.org /transcripts/2011/06/17/04. You can read and download the full FCC report here: http://www.fcc.gov/info-needs-communities.

73. Spiro Kiousis, interview with the author, 1/20/2011. Professor Kiousis said this trend puts greater ethical responsibility on press agents.

74. Center for Media and Democracy, "Fake TV news, widespread and undisclosed," PRWatch.org, online at: http://www.prwatch.org/fakenews/findings/vnrs. During the presidency of George W. Bush, the federal government also participated in fake news.

75. Terry Gross (1/21/2012) "How SuperPacs are 'gaming' the 2012 campaign," Fresh Air, National Public Radio, online at: http://www.npr.org /templates/transcript/transcript.php?storyId=146137765.

76. In our last year-long grading sample of San Francisco Bay Area's most popular news media, all three papers received an A for fairness, three television stations earned Bs and two earned Cs. None failed the test of including at least one other side in stories involving controversy or accusations. We observed very little liberal or conservative bias. In fact, only one group was consistently treated unfairly, individuals arrested for violent crime rarely were given the chance to respond to allegations. You can see the full report at: http://www.gradethenews.org/feat/recentgrades/2004.htm.

77. Walter Lippmann (1922) *Public Opinion*, reprinted in 1965 by Free Press, New York.

78. Anthony Downs (1957) *An Economic Theory of Democracy*, New York: Harper and Brothers. Downs wrote: The value of a single vote "is nearly infinitesimal under most circumstances.... The result is an enormously diminished incentive for voters to acquire political information before voting." p. 245.

Ch. 5: Setting Realistic Standards for Judging News and Information

1. By values I'm referring to preferences and dispositions of the kind described in chapters three and four, based on personal and institutional self-interest.

2. Otto Kerner and the National Advisory Commission on Civil Disorders (1968) *Report of the National Advisory Commission on Civil Disorders*, Washington, DC: U.S. Government Printing Office. Excerpt online at: http://historymatters.gmu.edu/d/6553/. Of white bias the Commission concluded: "This may be understandable, but it is not excusable in an institution that has the mission to inform and educate the whole of our society."

3. Quoted in Nick Davies (2009) *Flat Earth News*, London: Vintage Books, p. 44-45.

4. Cronkite was addressing the Radio and Television News Directors Convention on Dec. 13, 1976, quoted in Marvin Barrett (1978) *Rich news, poor news: the sixth Alfred J. Dupont-Columbia University survey of broadcast journalism*, New York: Thomas Y. Crowell, p. 24.

5. Cunningham, Brent (July/August 2003) Re-thinking objectivity, *Columbia Journalism Review* Vol. 42, no. 2, pp. 24-32.

6. W. Lance Bennett, Regina G. Lawrence, and Steven Livingston (2007) *When the Press Fails: Political Power and the News Media from Iraq to Katrina*, Chicago: University of Chicago Press. This book contains an extended analysis of how objectivity norms led journalists to merely accept rather than question the Bush administration's claims that Iraq had weapons of mass destruction and that it had a role in the 9/11 terror attacks.

7. If journalists are to ask the questions of the community they serve, they must meet regularly with members throughout that community to learn their concerns and interests. As the former Knight Ridder news executive and publisher Larry Jinks puts it, "In determining what's important, the journalist needs to have real interaction with the members of the audience rather than simply determining it from on high." (Interview with the author on 6/16/2008).

8. Union of Concerned Scientists, "The Weight of the Evidence," online at: http://www.ucsusa.org/global_warming/science _and_impacts/science/weight-of-the-evidence.html. (Disclosure: I'm a contributor to the Union of Concerned Scientists.)

9. The economic origins of the objectivity standard have been written about by many scholars including Leon Sigal (1973) *Reporters and officials*, Lexington, MA: D.C. Heath; Michael Schudson (1978) *Discovering the News*, New York: Basic Books; Paul Starr (2004) *The creation of the media*, New York: Basic Books.

10. I confess that it is much easier to say that the selection of topics and the way they are covered should reflect the common good than it is to put it into practice. In hindsight, it's easy to see that African-Americans and women should have rights equal to those of white males. But what about contemporary controversies over rights: Do homosexual marriage rights serve the common good? Is their denial unjust? How about extending citizenship rights to minors whose parents illegally immigrated? The common good bias I'm advocating would thrust these topics into the news. It would also welcome respectful, fact-based arguments on all sides of the issues.

11. A claim that something is a fact requires that it can be proved true or false. In news, it's usually an assertion specific enough that it can be supported or undermined by evidence. If I say someone is a "terrible" governor, it's hard to know what I mean by "terrible," or how that might be proven true or false. On the other hand if I say the governor is an embezzler, one could check to see if s/he had been convicted of such a crime. Embezzlement has a specific meaning. Personal preferences and beliefs that cannot be shown to be true or false are not fact-claims; they are simply opinions. Opinions should never carry the same weight as fact in a controversy.

Ch. 6: The SMELL Test

1. The primary exception to this reduction of author and institution into a single blended source is for commentators who are experts themselves. Institutions allow considerable independence to guest experts who write op-ed articles and commentators with advanced degrees, such as a physician writing a medical column or a lawyer interpreting court decisions. In such cases, it's useful to evaluate the credibility of the commentator as well as the institution and the sources cited.

2. Carl Bernstein (7/18/2011) "Murdoch's Watergate," *Newsweek*, p. 5.

3. Some critics of journalism take an absolutist view: no unnamed sources should be allowed, period. But given how secretive – and vindictive -- corporations and government agencies have become, I think this is unrealistic. Reporters should always try to get sources to speak with full identification, even if they have to pass over some who wish to go unnamed. However, if a source with uniquely valuable information is both unwilling to go on the record and likely to suffer retribution if named, I think it's permissible to offer that source anonymity. But only if three other conditions are also met: 1) the reporter provides enough information for us to determine the source's proximity to the issue or event, his/er independence, and expertise/experience; 2) any accusations of mis- or malfeasance are independently confirmed by a second source; 3) to avoid being used as a shield for cheap shots, only fact-claims are permitted -- no opinions.

4. Shirley Lipschutz-Robinson (undated) "Vaccination: Deception and tragedy," online at: http://www.shirleys-wellness-cafe.com/vaccines.htm#1, accessed on 5/2/2011.

5. Public Broadcasting System, Frontline (May, 2010) "The vaccine war," online at: http://www.pbs.org/wgbh/pages/frontline/vaccines/view/.

6. Kerry Lauerman (1/16/2011) "Correcting our record," Salon.com, online at: http://www.salon.com/news/autism/index.html, (three quarters down the Web page.) Here's what Lauerman, the editor-in-chief at *Salon*, wrote about the Kennedy article:

In 2005, *Salon* published online an exclusive story by
Robert F. Kennedy Jr. that offered an explosive
premise: that the mercury-based thimerosal compound
present in vaccines until 2001 was dangerous, and that
he was 'convinced that the link between thimerosal and
the epidemic of childhood neurological disorders is real.'
The piece was co-published with *Rolling Stone* magazine -
- they fact-checked it and published it in print; we
posted it online. In the days after running 'Deadly
Immunity,' we amended the story with five corrections
(which can still be found at
http://www.salon.com/letters/corrections/2005/index.
html) that went far in undermining Kennedy's exposé.
At the time, we felt that correcting the piece -- and
keeping it on the site, in the spirit of transparency -- was
the best way to operate. But subsequent critics,
including most recently, Seth Mnookin in his book 'The
Panic Virus' further eroded any faith we had in the
story's value. We've grown to believe the best reader
service is to delete the piece entirely.

7. Google says it's constantly changing the criteria used to rank
relevant Web sites, but companies have had success gaming they
system to land on the first page of results, according to the *New
York Times*: David Segal (2/12/2011) "Dirty little secrets of search,"
New York Times, p. 1B, online at:
http://www.nytimes.com/2011/02/13/business/13search.html.

8. Gardiner Harris (3/26/2008) "Cigarette company paid for lung
cancer study," *New York Times*, p. A1, national edition, online at:
http://www.nytimes.com/2008/03/26/health/research/26lung.ht
ml?_r=1&ref=research&oref=slogin.

9. Bill Kreuger (9/9/2010) "Egg industry Website gets boost from
media during salmonella recall." Making sense of News,
PoynterOnline, available at: http://www.poynter.org/latest-
news/making-sense-of-news/105509/egg-industry-website-gets-
boost-from-media-during-salmonella-recall/.

10. The most prominent exception I can think of is Ira Glass' This
American Life on NPR, which introduces a sound track under the
narration.

11. Clark Hoyt (6/1/2008) "Entitled to their opinions, yes. But their facts?" *New York Times* Week in Review section p. 12.

12. Gail Collins (1/29/2012) "Newt's real legacy," Sunday Review, *New York Times*, p. 1SR.

13. Politifact.com (9/13/2011) "Truth-o-meter: Mitt Romney and the dog on the car roof: one columnist's obsession," online at: http://www.politifact.com/truth-o-meter/statements/2011/sep/13/gail-collins/mitt-romney-and-dog-car-roof-one-columnists-obsess/.

14. Brooks Jackson and Kathleen Hall Jamieson (2007) *Unspun*, New York: Random House, p. 26.

15. News staff, *Science 2.0* (10/12/2008) "There's An Expert On The Political Effects Of Late-Night Comedy - And She Says Tina Fey Hurts McCain's Campaign," online at: http://www.science20.com/ news_releases /theres_an_expert_on_the_political_effects_of_late _night_comedy_and_she_says_tina_fey_hurts_mccains_campaign.

16. Jessica G (10/13/2008) "Tina Fey is on her way 'to ruining Sarah Palin's political career'," Jezebel.com

17. Heather A. Dean (summer, 2010) "'I can see Russia from my house: Tina Fey's impersonation of Sarah Palin as a template for media coverage in the 2008 presidential election,'" master's thesis, San Diego State University, available online at: http://sdsu-dspace.calstate.edu/xmlui/bitstream/ handle/10211.10/461/Dean_Heather.pdf?sequence=1.

18. Jon Stewart (4/20/2010) The Daily Show, responding to an attack by Bernard Goldberg on Fox News' O'Reilly Factor. Stewart has frequently criticized the news media for mixing too much entertainment in newscasts, e.g. (10/31/2010) Final speech at the Rally to Restore Sanity in Washington, DC, online at: http://www.youtube.com/watch?v=6JzGOiBXeD4.

19. Ohio History Central (undated) "Uncle Tom's Cabin," Ohio Historical Association's online encyclopedia of Ohio history, available online at: http://www.ohiohistorycentral.org/entry.php?rec=1405, accessed 5/23/2011.

20. David S. Reynolds (6/14/2011) "Rescuing the real Uncle Tom," *New York Times*, p. A21 online at: http://www.nytimes.com/2011/06/14/opinion/14Reynolds.html?_r=1&hp.

21. The relationship between entertainment and news is complicated. High quality news media use drama to make what's important interesting. They may also properly include a few articles that are simply amusing to build audience for more serious fare. But when the proportion of "cotton candy" stories reaches double digits, the news provider risks displacement of the consequential for the merely compelling. The phrase "weapons of mass distraction" was originated by MASH producer Larry Gelbart and used as the title of a 1996 HBO movie. It originally referred to TV.

22. Jon Stewart (10/31/2010) cited above.

23. Anderson Cooper (11/4/2010) "Keeping them honest: The $200 million myth," CNN online at: http://ac360.blogs.cnn.com/2010 /11/05/kth-the-200-million-myth-about-obamas-asia-trip/.

24. Project for Excellence in Journalism, (4/12//2010) "News leaders and the future," pp. 2-4, online at: http://www.journalism.org/analysis_report/news_leaders_and_future.

25. In discussion with the author (6/17/08)

26. Stephen Kull, Ramsey Clay and Evan Lewis (Winter, 2003) "Misperceptions, the media, and the Iraq war," *Political Science Quarterly*, vol. 118, no. 4, pp. 569-598; online at http://65.109.167.118/pipa/pdf/oct03/IraqMedia_Oct03_rpt.pdf.

27. Kull, Clay and Lewis study cited above.

28. Michael R. Gordon and Judith Miller (9/8/2002) "Threats and responses: the Iraqis; U.S. says Hussein intensifies quest for a-bomb parts," online at: http://www.nytimes.com/2002/09/08/world/threats-responses-iraqis-us-says-hussein-intensifies-quest-for-bomb-parts.html.

29. John McManus (7/1/2000) "How to read political polls like a pro," Grade the News, online at: http://www.gradethenews.org/dreamhost%20files /pagesfolder/Pollstory3.htm.

30. Jim Rutenberg, Marilyn W. Thompson, David D. Kirkpatrick, and Stephen Labaton (2/21/2008) "For McCain, self-confidence on ethics poses its own risk," *New York Times*, p. A1, online at: http://www.nytimes.com/200 8/02/21/us/politics/21mccain.html ?scp=1&sq=Vicki%20Iseman&st=cse.

31. Clark Hoyt (2/24/2008) "What that McCain article didn't say," *New York Times*, Week in Review section, online at: http://www.nytimes.com/2008/02/24/opinion/24pubed.html?sq= Vicki%20Iseman&st=cse&scp=7&pagewanted=all.

32. Jesse Jackson (1994) quoted in Sheldon R. Gawiser and G. Evans Witt, *A Journalist's Guide to Public Opinion Polls*, Westport, CT: Praeger, p. 111

33. Sheryl Gay Stolberg, Shaila Dewan and Brian Stelter (7/21/2010) "With apology, fired official is offered a new job," *New York Times*, p. A15, online at: http://www.nytimes.com/2010/07/22/us/politics/22sherrod.html.

34. Kate Phillips (3/27/2008) "McCain said '100': Opponents latch on," *New York Times*, p. A22.

35. Ethan Bronner (3/28/2012) "2 Israeli leaders make the Iran issue their own," *New York Times* p. A1, national edition.

36. Dean Buonomano (2011) *Brain bugs: How the brain's flaws shape our lives*, New York: W.W. Norton.

37. Drucilla Dyess (5/18/2011) "Coffee: New Wonder Drug Found to Cut Prostate Cancer Risk," Healthnews.com, online at: http://www.healthnews.com/Categories/Family-Health/Coffee-New-Wonder-Drug-Found-to-Cut-Prostate-Cancer-Risk.

38. Neil Conan (10/11/2011) Talk of the Nation, interview with Edward Schumacher-Matos, online at: http://www.npr.org/2011/10/11/141240659/npr-ombudsman-ponders-journalisms-big-questions. Quote is half way down transcript.

39. Rob Stein (11/3/2008) "Study first to link TV sex to real teen pregnancies," *Washington Post*, p. A1, online at: http://www.

washingtonpost.com/wp-dyn/content/article/2008/11/02/
AR2008110202592_pf.html.

40. Lee Ross (1977). "The intuitive psychologist and his
shortcomings: Distortions in the attribution process." in L.
Berkowitz Ed., *Advances in experimental social psychology* (vol. 10, pp.
173–220). New York: Academic Press.

41. Dale T. Miller and Michael Ross (1975) "Self-serving biases in
the attribution of causality: Fact or fiction?" *Psychological Bulletin* 82
(2): 213–225.)

42. Michael J. Sandel (2009) *Justice: What's the right thing to do?* New
York: Farrar, Straus and Giroux, p. 18. The CEO salary data earlier
in the paragraph also came from here.

43. See Lee Ross, cited above.

44. See, for example, the social ecology approach pioneered by the
Chicago School, e.g., Clifford R. Shaw and Henry D. McKay (1942)
Juvenile Delinquency and Urban Areas, The University of Chicago Press;
Gary Becker, "Crime and Punishment," in *Journal of Political Economy*,
vol. 76 (2), March–April 1968, p.196-217; and R. Kornhauser (1978)
Social Sources of Delinquency, Chicago: University of Chicago Press.

45. John McManus and Lori Dorfman (2005) "Functional truth or
sexist distortion," *Journalism*, 6(1): 43-65.

46. See Ellen Hume (2003). "Talk show culture," *Encyclopedia of
International Media and Communications*, Vol. 4 available online at:
http://www.ellenhume.com/articles/talkshow1.htm; also John
Halpin, James Heidbreder, Mark Lloyd, Paul Woodhull, Ben Scott,
Josh Silver, and S. Derek Turner (6/20/2007) "The Structural
Imbalance of Political Talk Radio," available online at:
http://www.americanprogress.org/issues/2007/06/talk_radio.html.

47. Wikipedia (undated) "Incarceration in the United States," online
at: http://en.wikipedia.org/wiki/Incarceration_in_the_
United_States, accessed 7/6/2011.

48. Maya Harris (5/29/2007) "Prison vs. education spending reveals
California's priorities," SFGate.com,http://articles.sfgate.com/2007-
05 -29/opinion/17244077_1_school-dropouts-school-diploma-

spending-on-higher-education. SFGate is the *San Francisco Chronicle's* Web site.

49. John Pomfret (6/11/2006) "California's crisis in prison systems a threat to public," *Washington Post*, available online at: http://www. washingtonpost. com/wp-dyn/content/article/2006/06/10/ AR2006061000719.html.

50. Michelle Alexander (2012) *The new Jim Crow: mass incarceration in the age of colorblindness*, New York: New Press.

51. John Pomfret (6/27/2006) "California prison system in 'crisis,' governor says," *Washington Post*, available online at: http://www. washingtonpost.com/ wp-dyn/content/article/2006/06/26/ AR2006062601240.html.

52. David Lague (3/18/2008) "China premier blames Dalai Lama for 'appalling' violence in Tibet," *New York Times*, online at: http://www.nytimes.com/2008/03/18/world/asia/18tibet.html?sc p=42&sq=chinese%20suprression%20of%20news%20about%20Ti bet&st=cse and (3/18/2008) "China tries to thwart news reports from Tibet," *New York Times*, at: http://www.nytimes.com /2008/03/18/ world/asia/18access.html?ref=asia.

53. Michael Massing (1/29/2004) "Now they tell us," *New York Review of Books*, available online at: http://www.nybooks.com/ articles/archives /2004/feb/26/now-they-tell-us/?pagination=false.

Ch. 7: Detecting Bias in Images

1. In this paragraph I'm relying on the following three Wikipedia sources: 1) "Anatomically modern humans," online at: http://en.wikipedia.org/wiki/ Anatomically_modern_humans# Modern_human_behavior; 2) "Rock art," at: http://en.wikipedia .org/wiki/Rock_art#Age; and 3) "Earliest writing," at http://en. wikipedia.org/wiki/Earliest_writing. All were accessed on 8/22/2011.

2. Here I'm relying on Neil Postman (1985) *Amusing ourselves to death*, New York: Penguin; Arthur Asa Berger (2008) *Seeing is believing*, New York: McGraw-Hill ; D. A. Dondis (2000) *A primer of visual literacy*,

Cambridge, MA: MIT Press; Joshua Meyrowitz (1998) "Multiple media literacies," *Journal of Communication*, vol. 48, no. 1, pp. 96-108; Herbert Zettl (1998) "Contextual media aesthetics as the basis for media literacy," *Journal of Communication*, vol. 48, no. 1, pp. 81-95; and Paul Messaris (1998) "Visual aspects of media literacy," *Journal of Communication*, vol. 48, no. 1, pp. 70-80.

3. Nick Ut, an *Associated Press* photographer, won a Pulitzer Prize for his June 1972 picture of a screaming girl burned with napalm. He also helped get the girl to a hospital, where she spent the next 14 months and, against odds, survived.

4. The Museum of Broadcast Communications (undated) "Vietnam on television," online at: http://www.museum.tv/eotvsection.php?entrycode=vietnamonte. Accessed 6/3/2011

5. Julian E. Barnes (2/27/2009) "Pentagon lifts media ban on photos of war dead," *Los Angeles Times*, online at: http://articles.latimes.com/2009/feb/27/nation/na-war-dead-photos27.

6. Harold A. Innis (1991; original 1951) *The bias of communication*, Toronto: University of Toronto Press. Marshall McLuhan (1994; original 1964) *Understanding media: the extensions of man*, Cambridge, MA: MIT Press.

7. Mihaly Csikszentmihalyi and Robert Kubey (1981) "Television and the rest of life: a systematic comparison of subjective experience," *Public Opinion Quarterly*, 45 (3): 317-328.

8. Hany Farid (undated) "Digital doctoring: Can we trust photographs?" Dartmouth College Library, pdf version available at: http://www.ists.dartmouth.edu/library/327.pdf. Accessed on 1/18/2012.

9. Bill Moyers (11/22/1989) "Illusions of news," second part of the series "The public mind," interview with Michael Deaver, Public Broadcasting Service, Washington, DC.

10. Scott Baker (3/10/2011) "Does raw video of NPR expose' reveal questionable editing & tactics?" TheBlaze.com, available at: http://www.theblaze.com/stories/does-raw-video-of-npr-expose-reveal-questionable-editing-tactics/.

11. San Francisco State Professor Arthur Asa Berger suggests compiling a broader list of opposite roles played by principal stakeholders in the photo: for example, who is portrayed as honest/devious, powerful/weak, or wealthy/poor.

12. Michael Schwirtz (11/6/2008) "Georgia fired more cluster bombs than thought, killing civilians, report finds," *New York Times,* p. A18, online at: http://www.nytimes.com/2008/11/ 06/world/europe/06cluster.html?ref=europe] and C.J. Chivers and Ellen Barry (11/6/2008) "Georgia claims on Russia war called into question," *New York* Times, p. A1, online at: :http://www.nytimes. com/2008/11/07/world/europe/07georgia.html?_r=1&scp=1&sq =Georgia%20Claims%20on%20Russia%20War%20Called%20Into %20Question&st=cse.

13. John Fiske (1987) *Television culture: Popular pleasures and politics,* New York, Methuen.

Ch. 8: The Spinmeister's Art: Tricks of the Misinformation Trade

1. Robert W. McChesney and John Nichols (2010) *The death and life of American journalism*, Philadelphia: Nation Books. The authors use data from the U.S. Bureau of Labor Statistics to estimate that the ratio of public relations practitioners to journalists has changed from approximately 1 to 1 in 1980 to more than three to one in 2008.

2. David Carr (12/10/2007) "Muckraking pays, just not in profit," *New York Times,* p. C1, online at: http://www.nytimes.com /2007/12/10/ business/media/10carr.html?_r=1&oref=slogin.

3. John Sullivan (May/June 2011) "True enough: the second age of PR," *Columbia Journalism Review*, pp. 34-39, available online at: http://www.cjr.org/feature/true_enough.php.

4. W. Dale Nelson (1998) *Who speaks for the president? The White House press secretary from Cleveland to Clinton.* Syracuse, NY: Syracuse University Press.

5. As their ability to shape public discourse has grown, publicists have sought to justify and gain respect for their craft by comparing

themselves to lawyers. Attorneys advocate for their clients in courts of law and public relations "counsels" advocate for theirs in the "court" of public opinion. But it's like comparing an apple to a road apple.

Unlike a court of justice, in the court of public opinion there are no rules of evidence, nothing to prevent hearsay or rumor. No counsel is appointed to ensure a fair hearing for those unable to afford representation. There are no hand-on-bible oaths to speak truth under penalty of perjury. In fact, there is no law against lying to the public. In the court of public opinion there is no judge to referee the matter and insist each side have its full say. There is no power to compel testimony or the production of documents, or to protect vulnerable witnesses from reprisal. And there is no jury of peers listening intently, only a distracted public paying occasional attention. None of the protections against half-truths and deception, nor the enhancements for seeking truth that characterize courts of law exist in the wild and wooly infosphere that shapes public opinion.

6. Bob Garfield (10/28/2011) "Is transparency always a good thing?" On the Media, National Public Radio.

7. Paul Mcleary (4/18/2005) "Money for nothing, and the news ain't free," *Columbia Journalism Review*, available online at: http://www. cjr.org/politics/money_for_nothing_and_the_news.php.

8. Zachary Roth (10/13/2004) "Video news releases – they're everywhere," *Columbia Journalism Review*, available online at: http://www.cjr.org/behind_the_news/video_news_releases_theyre _eve.php.

9. Wikipedia (accessed 6/3/2011) "Iraqi aluminum tubes," online at: http://en.wikipedia.org/wiki/Iraqi_aluminum_tubes.

10. Frontline (3/24/2008) "Bush's war," Public Broadcasting System. The "Meet the Press" clip is in Part one, ch. 11, approximately between 3:45 minutes and 5:05; See: http://www.pbs.org/wgbh/pages/frontline /bushswar/.

11. David Barstow (4/20/2008) "Message machine; Behind TV analysts, Pentagon's hidden hand," *New York Times*, p. A1; available online at: http://query.nytimes.com/gst/fullpage

.html?res=9501E7DF103CF933A15757C0A96E9C8B63&scp=1&s
q=Pentagon+and+news+consultants&st=nyt.

12. John Sullivan, referenced above, p. 34.

13. Wikipedia (accessed 5/26/2011) "Death panel," online at:
http://en.wikipedia.org/wiki/Death_panel.

14. Glenn Kessler (3/4/2011) "Democrats keep misleading on
claimed budget 'cuts'," *Washington Post*, available online at:
http://voices.washington post. com /fact-checker/2011/03/
democrats_keep_misleading_on_c.html.

15. Naomi Oreskes (1/24/2012) "Op-ed: The verdict is in on
climate change," Talk of the Nation with Neal Conan, National
Public Radio. Also see Jane Mayer (8/30/2010), "Covert
operations," *The New Yorker*, pp. 60-63; and Juliet Schor
(3/20/2011) "Who's really upset?" *New York Times* online feature,
Room for Debate at: http://www.nytimes.com/roomfordebate
/2011 /03/17/the-politicized-light-bulb/whos-really-upset-with-
energy-efficient-products?scp=1&sq=climate%20change%20
deniers%20and%20tobacco&st=cse.

16. Stanton A. Glantz, John Slade, Lisa A. Bero, Peter Hanauer, and
Deborah E. Barnes, Eds. (1996) *The cigarette papers*. Berkeley:
University of California Press; available online at:
http://ark.cdlib.org/ark:/13030/ft8489p25j/.

17. Philip M. Taylor (1995) "War and the media," address at the
British Royal Military Academy at Sandhurst. Mr. Taylor is a
professor at the Institute of Communications Studies at the
University of Leeds, UK, available online at: http://ics.leeds.ac.
uk/papers/vp01.cfm?outfit=pmt&folder=34&paper=39.

18. *Time Magazine* (2/12/1973) "The press: Farewell to the follies,"
available online at: http://www.time.com/time/magazine/article
/0,9171,903831,00.html#ixzz1dEbsaCEH.

19. Before trial, the soldier suspected of giving classified documents
to Wikileaks, Pvt. Bradley Manning, was kept in solitary
confinement and subjected to harsh imprisonment. See David
Leigh (3/16/2011) "You can hear Bradley Manning coming because
of the chains," *The Guardian*, available online at: http://www.

guardian .co.uk/media/2011/mar/16/hear-bradley-manning-because-chains.

20. Twainquotes.com (accessed on 8/11/2011) online at: http://www.twainquotes.com/Lies.html.

21. Wikipedia (accessed on 6/3/2011) "Enron," online at: http://en.wikipedia.org/wiki/Enron.

22. John Sullivan, referenced above, p. 36.

23. My thinking has been most shaped by George Lakoff (1996) *Moral politics*, Chicago: University of Chicago Press; Vincent Price and David Tewksbury (1997) "News values and public opinion: A theoretical account of media priming and framing," in *Progress in Communication Sciences*, Eds. George Barnett and Franklin J. Boster, Greenwich, CT: Ablex, pp. 173-212; and Stephen D. Reese (2001) "Prologue: Framing public life: A bridging model for media research," in Stephen D. Reese, Oscar H. Gandy Jr. and August E. Grant, Eds. *Framing public life*, Mahwah, NJ: Lawrence Erlbaum.

24. Wikipedia (accessed 6/6/2011) "Upper Big Branch mine disaster," online at: http://en.wikipedia.org/wiki/Upper_Big_Branch_Mine_disaster.

25. Glenn Kessler (1/10/2012) "Political Fact-checking under fire," Talk of the Nation, NPR, available online at: http://www.npr.org/2012/01/10/ 144974110/political-fact-checking-under-fire.

26. The Field Institute (2/29/2000) "Prop. 22 still running ahead," Berkeley, CA: University of California Data Archive.

27. Dean Buonomano (2011) *Brain bugs: How the brain's flaws shape our lives*, New York: W.W. Norton.

28. Sam Stein (8/3/2008) "Gergen: McCain using code words to attack Obama as 'uppity,'" *Huffington Post*, online at: http://www.huffington post.com/2008/08/03/gergen-mccain-is-using-co_n_116605.html.

29. Terrorism is a tactic – trying to achieve a political goal by instilling fear in a population through violence against civilians –

rather than a side in a conflict. Both states and insurgent groups can employ terror to gain their ends.

30. Sean Webby and Roxanne Stites (2/28/2001) "Man's failed marriage to Russian bride was prelude to fatal shooting," *San Jose Mercury News*, p. A1.

31. John McManus (3/10/2001) "Is wife-beating ever a love story?," Grade the News, online at: http://gradethenews.org/dreamhost%20 files/pagesfolder/Mcgovern1.htm.

32. *Frontline* (March 2008) "Bush's War" Part 1, Public Broadcasting System, online at: http://www.pbs.org/wgbh/pages/frontline/bushswar/.

Ch. 9: Online Tools for Sniffing Out Bias, Including Our Own

1. Wikipedia (accessed on 6/13/2011) "Socrates," online at: http://en.wikiquote.org/wiki/Socrates. Socrates agreed to take his own life rather than give up his philosophical inquiries about the wisdom of prominent Athenians.

2. Joyce Oldham Appleby (2003) *Thomas Jefferson* , New York: Times Books, p. 140.

3. Joel Williamson (1984) *The crucible of race: black/white relations in the American South since emancipation*, New York: Oxford University Press, p. 24.

4. Stanley Nelson, Director (5/16/2011) "Freedom Riders," The American Experience, Public Broadcasting System, available online at: http://www.pbs.org/wgbh/americanexperience/freedomriders/.

5. The editors of Time-Life Books (1991) *The Enterprise of War*, Alexandria, VA: Time-Life Books.

6. Jeffrey M. Jones (8/ 4/ 2008) "Majority of Americans Say Racism Against Blacks Widespread," Gallup Poll, Princeton, NJ, online at: http://www.gallup.com/poll/109258/majority-americans-say-racism-against-blacks-widespread.aspx.

7. Bob Garfield (4/29/2011) interview with James Fallows, "The birth certificate and legacy of presidential rumors," On the Media, NPR, online at: http://www.onthemedia.org/transcripts/2011/04/29/07.

8. Sally Lehrman (2007) "Believing is seeing: Optical illusions and social stereotypes," Poynter Online: http://www.poynter.org/column.asp?id=101&aid=130118.

9. Christopher Callahan and Leslie-Jean Thornton (2007) *A journalist's guide to the Internet*, Boston: Pearson, p. 30.

10. Snopes.com (6/20/2009) "Oliver Twisted" at: http://www.snopes.com/rumors/north.asp

11. Cary Spivak (December/January 2011) "The fact-checking explosion," *American Journalism Review*, available online at: http://www.ajr.org/article_printable.asp?id=4980.

12. David Streitfeld (8/19/2011) "In a race to out-rave, 5-star Web reviews go for $5," *New York Times*, p. A1, available online at: http://www.ny times.com/2011/08/20/technology/finding-fake-reviews-online.html.

13. David Segal (5/21/2011) "A rave or pan or just a fake," The Haggler, NewYorkTimes.com, online at: http://www.nytimes. com /2011/05/22/yourmoney/22haggler.html?_r=1&ref=thehaggler.

14. David Segal (2/26/2011) "But who will grade the grader?" The Haggler, NewYorkTimes.com, online at: http://www.nytimes .com/2011/02/27/your-money/27haggler.html?scp=1&sq= fraudulent+consumer+reviews&st=nyt.

15. Although the Huffington Post did win a Pulitzer Prize in 2012 for national reporting.

16. Michael Stoll and John McManus (2/1/2005) "Bay Area newspapers chose more trivial stories, but still beat local newscasts, 2003-04 grades show," Grade the News, online at: http://www.gradethenews.org/feat/recentgrades/2004.htm.

17. Stephen Waldman (2011) "The information needs of communities," Federal Communications Commission; chapter 3 on

television is available online at: http://transition.fcc.gov/osp/inc-report/INoC-3-TV.pdf. The entire report is available as a download at: http://transition.fcc.gov/osp/inc-report/The_Information_Needs_of_Communities.pdf

18. Pew Research Center for the People and the Press (9/12/2010) "Ideological News Sources: Who Watches and Why," online at: http://people-press.org/files/legacy-pdf/652.pdf. Other surveys with differently phrased questions shuffle the order. For example, an organization called Public Policy Polling conducted a survey in January 2010 resulting in much lower trust figures, but led by Fox with 49 percent, 10 points ahead of second place CNN. See Andy Barr (1/27/10) "Poll: Fox most trusted name in news," Politico.com, online at: http://www.politico.com/news/stories /0110/32039.html.

19. Brooke Gladstone (2/17/2012) "The changing nature of knowledge in the Internet age," interview with David Weinberger, author of *Too big to know*, On the Media, NPR, online at: http://www.onthemedia.org/ 2012/feb/17/changing-nature-knowledge-internet-age/transcript/.

20. Staff (6/30/2011) "Edelstein: Hamas member in flotilla shows intent to provoke," Jpost.com, online at: http://www.jpost.com/Headlines/Article.aspx?id=227349.

21. Lawrence Davidson (7/11/2011) "On flotillas and the law: Civil society versus Israel lobbies in US and Europe," Al-Jazeerah, online at: http://www.aljazeerah.info/Opinion%20Editorials /2011/July/11%20o/On%20Flotillas%20and%20the%20Law,%20 Civil%20Society%20Versus%20Israel%20Lobbies%20in%20US%2 0and%20Europe%20By%20Lawrence%20Davidson.htm.

22. A useful resource for locating international news sources is The News Directory: http://www.newsdirectory.com/index.php. Some international news sources in English include:

-- Agence France-Presse http://www.afp.com/english/home/

-- *Al-Ahram* (Egypt) http://weekly.ahram.org.eg/index.htm

-- Al Jazeera (Qatar) http://english.aljazeera.net/

-- *Asahi Shimbun* (Japan) http://www.asahi.com/english/english.html

-- BBC (United Kingdom) http://www.bbc.co.uk/

-- *Buenos Aires Herald* (Argentina) http://www.buenosairesherald.com/

-- CBC (Canada) http://www.cbc.ca/news/

-- *China Daily* http://www.chinadaily.com.cn/

-- *Copenhagen Post* (Denmark) http://www.cphpost.dk/

-- *Corriere della Sera* (Italy) http://www.corriere.it/english/

-- *Daily Star* (Lebanon) http://www.dailystar.com.lb/

-- Deutsche Welle (Germany) http://www.dw-world.de/dw/0,266,00.html

-- *Guadalajara Reporter* (Mexico) http://guadalajarareporter.com/

-- *The Guardian* (Nigeria) http://www.ngrguardiannews.com/

-- *The Guardian* (U.K.) http://www.guardian.co.uk/

-- *Haaretz* (Israel) http://www.haaretz.com/

-- Japan Today http://www.japantoday.com/

-- *Le Monde Diplomatique* (France) http://mondediplo.com/

-- *Moscow Times* (Russia) http://www.moscowtimes.ru/index.htm

-- *The Nation* (Pakistan) http://www.nation.com.pk/

-- *Spiegel* Online (Germany) http://www.spiegel.de/international/

-- *The Standard* (Kenya) http://www.eastandard.net/

-- *Today's Zaman* (Turkey) http://www.todayszaman.com/tz-web/

-- *Toronto Star* (Canada) http://www.thestar.com/

-- *Tehran Times* (Iran) http://www.tehrantimes.com/

-- *The Times of India* http://timesofindia.indiatimes.com/

-- *The Times of London* (U.K.)
http://www.timesonline.co.uk/tol/news/

23. I couldn't locate a similar option on Yahoo or Bing.

24. Walter Lippmann (1920) *Liberty and the News*, New York: Harcourt, Brace and Howe, p. 11 in Kindle version.

Index

InfoPlease.com 178
Infotainment 100, 105-6
Innis, Harold 129
Innuendo 113-5
Inskeep, Steve 45
Internet 1-5 (also see World
Wide Web)
Iraq
-- insurgency 53, 64-5, 115, 117
-- invasion 10-11, 58-9, 111-12,
123, 135, 146-7, 149, 151, 153,
156-9
Israeli-Palestinian conflict 36-
38, 182-3

J-Lab 56
Jackson, Brooks 103
Jackson, Jesse 115
Jamieson, Kathleen Hall 7, 103
Jefferson, Thomas 163-4
Jennings, Peter 8, 78
Jesus of Nazareth 14-5, 22-3
Journalism
-- autonomy of journalists 48
-- citizen 5, 55-7
-- consolidation of ownership
54-5
-- credibility 45, 70, 92, 94-8,
100, 107, 169, 175-6
-- demise of professional 2, 5-6,
51-55
-- diversity of staff 42, 44, 79-
80
-- economics 5-6, 51-5, 82
-- junk 76
-- local TV 66-7, 71, 74, 124
-- market pressures on 47-51
-- new sources 49
-- pandering 46, 57-60
-- role of entertainment 62, 68-
9, 76-7, 105-6, 208
-- sensationalism 52-4, 60-9
-- social value 12

-- staff workload 73-5

Kardashians 61
Kazmaier, Dick 23-4
Keeping Them Honest (CNN) 9,
108-9, 171
Kennedy, Robert F. Jr. 97
Kerger, Paula 65
Kessler, Glenn 148, 154, 171
Key, Pam 136
King, Martin Luther 2, 31
Kiousis, Spiro 73-4
Knight Foundation, John S. and
James L. vii, 1-2, 56
Knight Commission on the
Information Needs of
Communities in a Democracy 1-2,
185
Knight Ridder 56, 70
Koppel, Ted 56
KQED viii, 175
Kristof, Nicholas 39
Ku Klux Klan 2
Kyl, John 15

Lakoff, George 155
Lehrman, Sally 166-7
Lessig, Lawrence 63
Lewis, Anthony 33
Liebling, A.J. 5
Liggett 99
Lincoln, Abraham 104, 131
Linked-In 181
Limbaugh, Rush 9, 59, 69, 108
Lippmann, Walter 77, 184
Logic failures common in media
accounts 111-22
Lohan, Lindsay 61
Los Angeles Times 63, 71-2, 174

MSNBC 59, 76, 175
Maddow, Rachel 59
Madison, James 9-10

Acknowledgments

Here are some of the people who shaped this book and its academic precursor, an e-textbook called *Detecting Bull: How to Identify Bias and Junk Journalism in Print, Broadcast, and on the Wild Web.*

One of the nation's leading media literacy researchers, Reneé Hobbs of the University of Rhode Island, read every page of *Bull*. So did former Knight Ridder publisher and news executive Larry Jinks who did his best to keep me honest. Media economist Stephen Lacy at Michigan State; Dr. Faith Rogow, founding president of the American Media Literacy Association; and Dr. Deborah Gump of the Committee of Concerned Journalists critiqued each chapter.

Professors Bella Mody and Michael McDevitt of the University of Colorado offered advice as did Professor Marilyn Greenwald of Ohio University and Professor Doug Underwood of the University of Washington. Professor John Durham Peters of the University of Iowa added his insights as did Professor Stephan Russ-Mohl of Università della Svizzera italiana. Prof. Judy Muller, former ABC and NPR journalist and now professor of journalism at the University of Southern California, offered comments on this new book. So did three friends: Shiloh Ballard, author Paul Bendix and attorney Pamela Cohen, the queen of commas.

Professor Charles D. Feinstein of Santa Clara University helped shape the chapter on truth, as did Swedish journalist Torbjörn von Krogh and Professor Theodore L. Glasser of Stanford. Professor Chris Paterson of the University of Leeds helped me think about ideology. Prof. Arthur Asa Berger of San Francisco State University assisted on visual literacy. Cognitive scientist George Lakoff of the University of

California, Berkeley taught me about framing. Dori J. Maynard, director of the Maynard Institute for Journalism Education, alerted me to the "Fault Lines" bias analysis pioneered by her father Robert Maynard. The late William F. "Bill" Woo helped me become more sensitive to the value of human interest in news during the time Grade the News was at Stanford. Credit is due them all, but blame is mine alone.

About the Author

A former journalist and communication professor, John McManus writes and lectures about changes in news media and their impact on democracy. His 1994 book, *Market-Driven Journalism: Let the Citizen Beware?* won the annual research award from the Society of Professional Journalists. So did his 2009 college textbook, *Detecting Bull: How to Identify Bias and Junk Journalism in Print, Broadcast and on the Wild Web.* In 2000, he founded GradeTheNews.org. Using *Consumer Reports* as a model, the project scientifically sampled the most popular newspapers and newscasts in the San Francisco Bay Area and rated them head-to-head on seven yardsticks of journalism quality. Grade the News was funded by the Gerbode, Knight and Ford Foundations and received both national and regional awards.

56385773R00134

Made in the USA
Lexington, KY
20 October 2016